THE
WEALTH SPARK

IGNITING YOUR PATH TO ABUNDANCE AND SUCCESS

JAMES PARKER

"This book will start you firmly on the path to stepping into your greater-yet-to-be. Take it in and be abundantly blessed."

Michael Bernard Beckwith

The Wealth Spark reminds us that while there are many measures of success, the true measurement of Real success is how well calibrated we are to the vibration of our inner being, our God-self, our Divine Mind. The principles and practices of a prosperous mindset and heart-set as outlined in this book will start you firmly on the path to stepping into your greater-yet-to-be. Take it in and be abundantly blessed.

Michael Bernard Beckwith

Founder & CEO, Agape International Spiritual Center

Author, Life Visioning and Spiritual Liberation & Host, Take Back Your Mind Podcast

Paperback ISBN 979-8-9891808-2-0

Ebook ISBN 979-8-9891808-3-7

Library of Congress - TXu 2-393-733

For more information about this book and other products visit https://thewealthsparkbook.com

DEDICATION

To the warriors of dreams, to the relentless hearts pulsing with ambition, to the daring souls who've tasted the grit of challenge and emerged stronger — this volume is your beacon.

To you who've stared into the eyes of adversity, laughed, and declared, "Is that all you've got?" — this blueprint of wealth creation is your sword and shield.

To you who believe in the magnificent allure of potential and the intoxicating promise of prosperity — may this book become more than mere paper and ink. Let it be the spark that ignites the wildfire of wealth within you; let it be your compass guiding you toward your treasure; let it be your catalyst transforming potentiality into tangibility.

Dare to dream. Dare to act. Dare to reach higher. Dare to conquer. This is your hour. This is your catalyst. The future of wealth is in your hands.

EPIGRAPH

"The real measure of your wealth is how much you'd be worth if you lost all your money."

— Anonymous

PREFACE

Behold! An adventure unfolds, sparked by a potent revelation: a single idea, a glimmering inspiration, or a transformative individual that can send ripples through the still waters of your financial life, becoming a veritable maelstrom of wealth creation.

The Wealth Spark is more than a simple guide to financial prosperity. It's a crusade, a journey, an exploration through the wilderness of human potential, relationships, and unwavering tenacity. It's the result of tireless research, unending curiosity, and decades immersed in the throes of fostering prosperity and building a wealth consciousness. It is a testament to my commitment to ignite the hidden fires of potential within you, to help you navigate the labyrinth of your physical, emotional, spiritual, and financial journey.

Inside these pages, there are no false promises of instant riches or overnight success. Instead, *The Wealth Spark* delivers the robust bedrock of enduring wealth: invaluable skills and knowledge, a strong and supportive network, a mindset of indomitable perseverance, and a rich tapestry of non-material wealth that underscores the joy and contentment of our human experience.

It's an incantation to the power of self-growth and lifelong learning, an affirmation of the wealth that resides in relationships, and a tribute to the strength that resides in every setback, every challenge faced. It acknowledges the wealth that cannot be quantified — time, health, happiness, experiences — riches that breathe life into your existence, bringing satisfaction and contentment regardless of your bank balance.

The Wealth Spark is a call to action, an invitation to step into the arena of your financial destiny. It emboldens you to dream with audacity, strive with tenacity, and unlock your boundless potential.

Now, stand at the precipice of transformation. Dare to peer into the vast expanse of the unknown. Leap into your unique journey of wealth creation.

Welcome to your odyssey. The future beckons, abundant with promise.

- Reverend James Parker

TABLE OF CONTENTS

Dedication -- iv

Epigraph --- v

Preface -- vi

Acknowledgments -- xi

Introduction --xv

Chapter I: Adopting a Wealth Mindset -------------------------------- 1

Chapter II: Habits of Successful People --------------------------------17

Chapter III: The Power of Visualization and Affirmations -------- 39

Chapter IV: Action: Attaining Abundance and Success ------------ 55

Chapter V: Living a Life of Abundance and Success --------------- 99

Chapter VI: Bringing It All Together ----------------------------- 117

Afterword -- 123

About the Author --- 127

ACKNOWLEDGMENTS

Creating *The Wealth Spark: Igniting Your Path to Abundance and Success* has been an exceptional journey, a labor of love, and a profound experience of personal growth. This endeavor would not have been possible without the unwavering support, endless inspiration, and immense wisdom of many significant individuals, cherished institutions, and beloved family members who have graced my life's path.

At the very heart of my journey are my beautiful children, Sheree (Patrice), Curran, Angel, Bianca (Bebe), and Jaime. Your love and faith in me have been my motivation, my rock, my compass. To my dear brothers and sisters, Daryl, Lottie Kay, Jake, Dorena (sister-in-law), and my deeply cherished and forever loved sister Denise (deceased), as well as my host of nieces and nephews, your encouragement, strength, and belief in me have been vital pillars in this endeavor. My cherished grandchildren, Syniah, Ronald James, Gabby, Bryson, and Elijah: each of you light up my world and fuel my resolve. To my remarkable parents, Jake and Magnolia, who have transitioned but left behind an enduring legacy and invaluable life lessons, you remain my guiding stars.

My god-sister Dina; extended family of aunts, uncles, and cousins across the globe; incredible friends, neighbors, classmates, students, church members, business and training partners, clients, counselees, mentees, and associates have each touched my life, inspiring and enriching it in their own unique ways.

I am deeply grateful for the mentorship and wisdom of esteemed colleagues including Gregory Guice, Jim Lee, James Trapp, Charline Manuel, Marianne Williamson, Shaheerah Stephens, Jim Blake, Shad Groverland, Derrick Wells, and the dearly departed Rev. Dr. Ruth Mosely, Rev. Johnnie Coleman, and Rev. Jack Boland.

My deepest appreciation goes to the spiritual organizations that have been my sanctuaries of learning and transformation: Unity Church in Chicago, Detroit Unity Temple, Christ Universal Temple, Westside Unity, Unity of Farmington Hills, Christ Unity Church of Ann Arbor, Renaissance Unity (Church of Today), Transforming Love Community, Lombard Mennonite Peace Center, Unity Urban Ministerial School, Unity Institute and Seminary, Unity World Headquarters, Unity Worldwide Ministries, G.L.U.R.C., and Truth Unity. Your teachings have been pivotal in shaping this book.

The contributions of organizations such as the Community Enterprise Non-Profit Corporation, Peterboro-Charlotte Historic Non-Profit, National Minority Business Development Corporation, City of Detroit Chamber of Commerce, and the American Anthropological Association have been invaluable, bolstering the evidence and credibility of the principles presented in this book.

To Carol Brewer, the remarkable team and dedicated staff of Unity Chicago, the Board of Trustees, Prayer Chaplains, Welcome Team, Spiritual Renewal and Education Committee, Hospitality, and the host of volunteers, musicians, and technicians across multiple organizations, your steadfast support has been instrumental. Special mention goes to my editor, Diane Valletta, and Stanley Robertson, whose expertise ensured this work reached its potential.

The wisdom of authors and scholars like Marianne Williamson, James Clear, Wallace D. Wattles, Napoleon Hill, Deepak Chopra, Norman Vincent Peale, Michael Norton, Elizabeth Dunn, Stephen Covey, Morgan Housel, Thomas J. Stanley, William Danko, George S. Clason, Viktor E. Frankl, Louise Hay, Georgiana Tree West, Charles and Myrtle Fillmore, Eric Butterworth, Jens O. Parsson, Don Miguel Ruiz, Kahlil Gibran, Ken Blanchard, Phil Hodges, Florence Shinn, and the guiding principles from the Holy Bible have been the intellectual foundations of this guide to abundance and success.

As I conclude, I wish to extend my gratitude to every person who has participated in this journey, however large or small, toward my life and this book. Your contributions, direct or indirect, have been instrumental in the creation of *The Wealth Spark*. You have not only inspired *The Wealth Spark*, but you have also contributed to my personal growth and understanding of the true essence of abundance and success.

Finally, to all my readers who are embarking on their own path to abundance and success, this work is dedicated to you. I pray *The Wealth Spark: Igniting Your Path to Abundance and Success* proves to be a resource that ignites and fuels your path to creating the life you aspire to live. As we journey together, I am reminded of a beautiful proverb that says, 'If you want to go fast, go alone. If you want to go far, go together.' Here's to our shared journey toward a life of abundance and success. Let us celebrate the power within us to create, to grow, and to contribute to the world in meaningful ways. Remember, we are all catalysts for wealth and success in our own unique ways. Your journey begins now. Ignite your path and shine your light brightly.

With deep appreciation, heartfelt thanks, love and blessings,

- **Reverend James Parker**

INTRODUCTION

Welcome to *The Wealth Spark: Igniting Your Path to Abundance and Success!* This book is your ultimate guide to reaching your deepest desires and realizing your full potential. In today's fast-paced world, attaining or manifesting abundance and success are more important than ever, and this book will help you develop the mindset, habits, and practices necessary for achieving them.

In today's globalized world, success can take many forms. Financial stability, career success, personal growth — whatever it may be for you — all these things can be considered success. No matter your definition, this book provides tools and guidance to help you get there.

Cultivating the right mindset is where the journey begins. This requires breaking free from limiting beliefs and negative self-talk and replacing them with thoughts of positivity and abundance. Building on mindset, the book provides practical advice to help you create beneficial habits and practices. It will guide you on your transformational journey toward the life you desire.

The Wealth Spark offers a clear and comprehensive blueprint to abundance and success. It is divided into four key sections, each outlining an essential aspect of attaining that success.

Creating a Wealth Mindset: This chapter will guide you through the process of liberating yourself from restrictive beliefs and negative self-talk, cultivating an attitude of gratitude that will aid in your success journey.

Cultivating Successful and Positive Habits and Practices: Here you'll gain practical tips and exercises to help you create positive habits and practices that will propel you toward abundance.

Taking Action: Here you'll find valuable tools for turning your dreams into reality by applying the steps, strategies, and practices outlined in this book.

Bringing It All Together for Sustained Success: Finally, this chapter offers guidance on how to maintain your newfound abundance and success over the long haul.

Throughout the book, you'll come across references to both modern and historical sources as well as quotes from thought leaders in abundance and success. These connections will give you a deeper understanding of the concepts presented and serve to motivate and inspire you on your journey.

Let *The Wealth Spark* be your guide to unlocking the secrets of abundance and success in today's globalized world. Whoever you are — whether a business professional, seeker on a spiritual path, or starting your own journey toward wealth accumulation — this book provides all the tools necessary for reaching your true potential and living the abundant life you have always desired.

CHAPTER I

ADOPTING A WEALTH MINDSET

Buckle up! This chapter takes you on an enlightening journey into the realms of the mind, illuminating the path to the prosperity you desire in your life. It serves as a treasure map, where the wealth mindset is the X that marks the spot. Here, you will navigate through the stark contrasts between this prosperous outlook and the confining mindset of scarcity, unearthing the psychological, emotional, and spiritual barriers that may have held you back.

As you will discover, the wealth mindset doesn't merely stop at acknowledging these restrictive beliefs; it arms you with practical strategies to confront and conquer them. By deploying these tactics, you disentangle yourself from any repeated or looming stuck, stiff, or stubborn self-limiting thoughts, creating a clearing for the seeds of abundance to flourish.

Today, there is abundant knowledge available on how to become wealthy and successful. From books and courses to seminars and online programs, the market offers a plethora of advice for financial abundance. Unfortunately, despite their best efforts, many people struggle to reach the level of wealth they desire, often due to lacking the necessary mindset or habits essential for true prosperity.

Wealth Mindset vs. Scarcity Mindset: What's the Difference?

At the core of this issue lies a distinction between a wealth mindset and a scarcity mindset. The former emphasizes abundance, possibility, and growth. It is the belief that opportunities are limitless and that success can be attained through hard work and determination. On the other hand, scarcity mindsets focus on lack, limitation, and fear, driven by the belief that there are only limited options available and that success belongs only to select individuals.

Among the greatest obstacles to developing a wealth mindset are limiting beliefs that may have been instilled from childhood experiences or social conditioning. These beliefs, such as money being evil, rich people being greedy, or success being only possible through luck or connections, can be devastating if not overcome.

Addressing limiting beliefs is like embarking on a transformative journey from the shadowy depths of scarcity to the radiant peaks of prosperity. It necessitates a courageous plunge into the depths of our self-perceptions to excavate and illuminate the obscure limiting beliefs that shackle us. This could be done through methods like introspective self-reflection, expressive journaling, or even by enlisting the assistance of a guide in the form of a coach or therapist.

Once these limiting beliefs have been identified and acknowledged, they become like misleading beacons that we can start to dissolve with the light of awareness and truth. For example, if you discover that you're carrying around the limiting belief that "money is evil," you can begin to dissolve this belief by challenging it with contrasting evidence.

Consider, for example, the story of Chuck Feeney. A self-made billionaire and co-founder of the Duty-Free Shoppers Group, Feeney believed so strongly in the power of philanthropy that he has given away nearly all his wealth, approximately $8 billion, to charitable causes. His contributions have funded advancements in education, science, and civil rights across the globe, inspiring a generation of high-wealth philanthropists including Bill Gates and Warren Buffet. In Feeney's story, we see the profound potential of wealth to be a powerful tool for good when guided by an enlightened perspective.

So, while the process of overcoming limiting beliefs might seem daunting at first, remember that it's a voyage toward personal liberation. Like a catalyst in a chemical reaction, challenging these beliefs can accelerate your journey from scarcity to prosperity, transforming your perspective, your life, and ultimately, your ability to manifest wealth.

The capacity for seeing possibilities instead of limitations is an essential characteristic of the wealth mindset. This means approaching challenges and obstacles with an upbeat outlook rather than becoming stuck in negativity or defeatism. Those who possess this outlook can spot opportunities where others only see roadblocks, and they take calculated risks in pursuit of their dreams.

One of the best ways to cultivate a wealth mindset is through consistent practice and repetition. This involves regularly engaging in activities that reinforce this mindset, such as visualization, affirmations, and gratitude practices. Visualization involves creating an image of desired outcome, while affirmations involve repeating positive statements to yourself. Gratitude exercises focus on appreciating what you are thankful for in life and expressing appreciation for those things.

In addition to these practices, it is essential to surround yourself with positive influences. This could include reading books or listening to podcasts from thought leaders in personal development and wealth creation; it could also involve seeking out like-minded individuals or groups who share similar ideals and principles.

Finally, cultivating a wealth mindset is critical for achieving true abundance and success. This requires overcoming limiting beliefs, focusing on possibilities instead of limitations, and engaging in consistent practices that promote this mindset. By adopting this perspective, you can create the conditions necessary for abundance to thrive in your life.

Marianne Williamson once said, "We were created to shine, just as children do. Our souls are meant to make manifest the glory of God that dwells within us — not just some of us but everyone. As we allow our own light to shine, we unconsciously give others permission to do the same. As we are liberated from our own fear, our presence automatically liberates others."

Cultivating a Wealth Mindset

Wealth and scarcity mindsets are not always associated with one's financial situation. People with a wealth mindset may have little money, while those with a scarcity mindset may possess plenty of assets. In the end, it is attitude and approach to life that ultimately determines outcome — not necessarily one's financial standing.

Attaining a wealth mindset requires effort and persistence, but it is achievable with the right attitude and approach. Here are some proven strategies.

Five Strategies for Cultivating a Wealth Mindset

1. Focus on Abundance: Think of this as always looking at the glass half full. By focusing on what you have — your skills, your assets, your opportunities — you'll find yourself noticing new ways to make money. This shift in perspective can help you spot investment opportunities, like a promising startup or a hot property, that you might have missed otherwise.

2. Be Eager to Learn and Grow: Never stop learning or trying to better yourself. This goes for your finances, too. Learn about different ways to invest, manage your money, and create income

without working more hours (this is what we call "passive income"). Financial mistakes aren't failures, they're lessons — as long as you learn from them, you'll keep getting better at managing your money.

3. Take Calculated Risks: Don't be scared to take a leap of faith with your money, but make sure you're not jumping blindfolded. Research, plan, and think it through before you invest in that promising business idea or buy those stocks. The people who are best at building wealth are not the ones who never take risks; they're the ones who take smart, thought-out risks.

4. Foster a Positive Outlook: Stay optimistic and always look for the silver lining. Even when your financial situation isn't looking great, stay positive and believe that you can turn it around. This positive attitude can help you make bold financial decisions, like investing in a bear market when others are selling off, which can be a key to achieving financial independence.

5. Express Gratitude: Take some time each day to appreciate what you have, whether that's your health, your family, or the roof over your head. Gratitude can help you feel secure and content with what you already have, and this calm mindset can make you a more rational, clearheaded decision-maker when it comes to your finances.

Remember, financial independence is not about becoming a millionaire overnight; it's about smart, consistent steps toward building and maintaining your wealth. Keep these principles in mind, and you'll be on the right track.

How a Scarcity Mindset Affects Finances

A scarcity mindset can have a detrimental effect on your finances. People with this attitude often fear loss, which leads to hoarding or overspending. Additionally, they may view money as a scarce resource that must be protected at all costs. Investing in personal development or business growth becomes less of an option, ultimately restricting one's capacity for creating wealth.

Conversely, those with a wealth mindset view money as an instrument to be used for creating more wealth. They are not afraid of taking risks and are willing to invest time and resources into their personal development and business growth, leading them down the path toward greater financial success in the long run.

The wealth mindset and scarcity mindset are two distinct ways of thinking that can profoundly influence your capacity for creating and maintaining wealth. Acquiring a wealth mindset takes effort and dedication, but it can be achieved with the right approach and attitude. By cultivating a wealth mindset, being open to learning and growth, taking calculated risks, maintaining a positive outlook, and showing gratitude, you can equip yourself with the skill set needed for financial success. It's essential to recognize the destructive effects of a scarcity mindset on your finances and to take steps to shift it toward abundance and growth. Remember, wealth doesn't just come from having money; it also involves having an upbeat outlook and being willing to invest in yourself and your future.

Limiting Beliefs and How to Overcome Them

As someone striving for abundance and success in all areas of my life, I have come to appreciate the significance of cultivating a wealth mindset. For me, this means cultivating positive thoughts that focus on possibilities instead of limitations or scarcity. It means dispelling any limiting beliefs that could be stopping me from reaching my objectives or realizing my full potential.

Limiting beliefs are negative thoughts or perceptions we hold about ourselves or the world around us that can become deeply embedded and prevent us from reaching our full potential. Fortunately, these limiting beliefs can be overcome and replaced with a wealth mindset.

The initial step in combating limiting beliefs is acknowledging them. I ask myself questions such as, "What negative beliefs do I hold about myself, my abilities, or the world around me?" "Do I believe that I'm not good enough or smart enough to achieve my goals?" and "Does the world seem harsh and unforgiving, where success only belongs to a select few?" By acknowledging these thoughts, I can begin challenging them and moving toward a wealth mindset.

Challenging limiting beliefs is no small undertaking. It requires courage to let go of negative thoughts that have been held onto for too long, yet it's an essential step in developing a wealth mindset. To test my limiting beliefs, I ask myself questions like, "Are these really true or simply negative thoughts I've been holding onto too long?" And then, "What evidence do I have to support or refute these beliefs?" By challenging my limiting thoughts, I can begin shifting my mindset and moving toward abundance and success.

Surrounding myself with positive influences is essential for cultivating a wealth mindset. By seeking out mentors or role models who exemplify the kind of mindset I wish to develop, I can begin shifting my way of thinking and dispelling limiting beliefs. Positive influences motivate and inspire me, keeping me focused on my objectives while helping me conquer any obstacles that come my way.

J. K. Rowling's story serves as a testament to her ability to overcome limiting beliefs. Before becoming famous as the author of *Harry Potter*, Rowling struggled as a single parent who had been rejected multiple times despite her ambition. Yet even in the face of these obstacles, Rowling never gave up on her ambition to become an author.

Rowling devised an effective strategy for conquering her limiting beliefs. She wrote herself a letter in which she imagined herself as an accomplished author with millions of fans, recounting the joy and fulfillment that success brought her. By visualizing success and believing in herself, Rowling was able to transcend her doubts and achieve greatness.

Rowling's story exemplifies the power of visualization and positive thinking. By believing in herself, she was able to overcome her limiting beliefs and reach her goals. This lesson has remained with me throughout my own life — a lesson that I believe is essential for developing a wealth mindset.

By acknowledging your limiting thoughts, challenging them, and surrounding yourself with positive influences, you can shift your perspective and unlock your full potential. J. K. Rowling's story serves as evidence that visualization combined with positive thinking can bring out the best in you; with determination you can overcome any limiting belief to reach your own greatness!

Toward an Uplifting, Abundance-Oriented Attitude

As someone committed to achieving abundance and success in all areas of my life, I've come to recognize that cultivating a wealth mindset is essential for reaching my objectives. A wealth mindset is an attitude of abundance, possibility, and positivity; it involves cultivating positive thinking, which allows me to see what's possible rather than what limits me.

To cultivate a wealth mindset, I have found it helpful to implement several techniques that keep me focused and optimistic. Here are some that have worked for me.

Five Abundance-Oriented Mindset Cultivation Techniques

1. **Gratitude Practice:** Expressing gratitude is one of the most effective techniques for cultivating an abundance-oriented mindset. By reflecting on what we are thankful for, we shift our focus from what we don't have to what we do have. Gratitude helps us feel contented with life's blessings while cultivating gratitude toward all God has provided us — as well as cultivating feelings of thankfulness toward ourselves!

I have discovered that regularly practicing gratitude has a powerful impact on my mindset. Every morning, I take a few minutes to reflect on what I am thankful for and write down three things in a journal — this simple act helps keep me focused on the positive aspects of life.

2. **Visualization:** The visualization technique involves creating an inner picture of our desired outcomes. This can be an invaluable aid in cultivating a wealth mindset, as it keeps us focused on our goals and inspires confidence that we will succeed.

   Visualization has proven to be a useful tool for me. I begin by defining my goals and creating an inspiring mental picture of what success will look like when they are achieved. Visualizing myself reaching these milestones fills me with joy as well as the euphoria that comes from reaching them. This technique keeps me focused on my objectives while motivating me to take action toward them.

3. **Positive Affirmations:** These are statements we repeat to ourselves to create a more optimistic and abundance-focused mindset. They are an effective way of reprogramming our subconscious mind so it focuses on what we desire instead of what we don't want.

   I have found that positive affirmations are most helpful when they are specific and related to my goals. For instance, if my objective is to launch a successful business, then repeating "I am a successful business owner" regularly gives me confidence in my abilities to reach them and helps keep me focused on what I want to achieve.

4. **Mindfulness:** An approach of mindfulness emphasizes being present and fully engaged in the present moment. It can help cultivate feelings of serenity and focus, which may be particularly helpful when developing a wealth mindset.

When practicing mindfulness, I make a point to focus on my breathing and let go of any distracting thoughts or worries. This helps me stay present in the moment and concentrate on whatever task is at hand — whether that be working on a project or spending quality time with family and friends — keeping me focused and calm even during stressful situations.

5. **Continuous Learning:** This involves continually seeking out new knowledge and skills to reach our objectives. It serves as an incentive to remain engaged and motivated throughout the process of success.

   I strive to learn continuously through reading books, attending seminars, and seeking out mentors who can support me in my growth and development. By remaining open to new ideas and perspectives while developing my skill set and knowledge base, I stay motivated and focused on my goals while being better prepared to tackle any obstacles that come my way. By continuously developing myself intellectually and practically, I gain the necessary tools for success — both professional and personal.

In addition to these techniques, I've found it beneficial to surround myself with positive and supportive people. Belonging to a group that believes in me and supports my goals has been instrumental in cultivating a wealth mindset. These individuals offer me encouragement when needed most, helping me stay motivated even when things get challenging.

Another key element in developing a wealth mindset is learning to let go of limiting beliefs. Limiting beliefs are those negative thoughts and perceptions that prevent us from reaching our objectives. Although they can be deeply embedded and difficult to alter, practice makes perfect, and it becomes possible to alter your perspective on life.

One inspiring story that comes to mind relative to letting go of limiting beliefs is Roger Bannister. Before his remarkable feat in 1954, many experts had believed it impossible for a human to run a mile in under four minutes; unfortunately, this belief had become so deeply embedded in society that many athletes never even attempted it.

But Bannister never gave up. He remained committed to his goal and working toward it until he broke through that long-elusive four-minute barrier on May 6, 1954, with a time of 3 minutes, 59.4 seconds. Bannister's success demonstrated that limiting beliefs are just that — beliefs. They can be conquered through hard work, determination, and an upbeat outlook.

Developing a wealth mindset is fundamental for achieving abundance and success in all aspects of our lives. By focusing on abundance, possibility, and positivity, we can cultivate an attitude that keeps us motivated toward our goals while believing in our capacity for achievement. Techniques such as gratitude practice, visualization, positive affirmations, mindfulness meditation, and continuous learning all help foster this mindset. And by letting go of limiting beliefs and surrounding ourselves with supportive people who motivate us along the way, we will conquer any challenges — no matter how large or small they may appear initially.

Practices for Developing a Wealth Mindset

In my journey toward the pursuit of abundance and success, I understand the significance of developing a wealth mindset. A wealth mindset is an attitude that emphasizes abundance, possibility, and positivity. It involves cultivating positive thinking that allows me to focus on what's possible instead of what limits me.

To cultivate a wealth mindset, I have found these practical exercises helpful in keeping me focused and upbeat.

Seven Practical Exercises for Wealth Mindset Development

1. Recognize Limiting Beliefs: The initial step is acknowledging any limiting beliefs that might be holding us back. These can be deeply held, making them difficult for us to identify on our

own; however, with practice we can become more aware of our thoughts and attitudes.

To identify limiting beliefs, pay attention to your thoughts and the language you use. When statements like "I can't do that" or "that's impossible" come to mind, take a moment to consider whether these statements reflect reality or are simply holding you back. Once it's been identified as a limiting belief, work on reframing it into something more positive and empowering.

For instance, when I find myself thinking "I can never save enough money," I can reframe the thought by affirming that "I am capable of saving money and possess the discipline to do so."

2. Practice Gratitude: Expressing gratitude is an effective exercise for cultivating a positive, abundance-oriented mindset. By reflecting on what you are grateful for in life, you shift your focus from what you don't have to what you already possess — cultivating an attitude of abundance and appreciation for life's blessings.

To cultivate gratitude, I make it a habit of taking a few moments each morning to reflect on what I am grateful for. Jotting down three things in my journal helps keep me focused on the positive aspects of life.

3. Create a Vision Board: Constructing a vision board is an enjoyable and creative exercise to help visualize goals and stay motivated to reach them. A vision board serves as a tangible visual representation of your aspirations, with images, words, and phrases that motivate you.

Create a vision board by collecting images and words that represent your goals and aspirations, then arranging them on an attractive board in an encouraging visual display. My board is kept visible at all times so I can see it daily, reminding me of my objectives.

4. **Foster a Wealth Mindset Through Visualization:** This effective technique involves creating mental images of your desired outcomes. Visualization keeps you focused on your goals and gives you confidence in achieving them.

   To visualize, I begin by identifying my goals and creating a mental picture of what success will look like when they are achieved. Visualizing myself achieving these objectives gives me immense pleasure, motivating me to take action toward them. Doing so keeps me focused on the task at hand while spurring me on toward greater achievement.

5. **Utilize Positive Affirmations:** By repeating positive affirmations to yourself, you can create a more upbeat and abundance-focused mindset. These statements can be an effective way of reprogramming your subconscious mind to focus on what you desire instead of what you don't want.

   Positive affirmations can help you stay focused on your objectives by being specific and aligned with them. For instance, if your goal is to improve your physical health and fitness, a positive affirmation could be: "I am becoming stronger and healthier every day." Or if your goal is overcoming stress and anxiety, a good affirmation could be: "I easily handle whatever comes my way, and I choose to feel calm and peaceful." Based on the need, repeating your chosen affirmations helps build your belief in your capacity for achieving your goals and keeps you motivated toward reaching them.

6. **Practice Mindfulness:** The mindfulness technique involves being present and aware of your thoughts, feelings, and environment. It's an invaluable tool in developing a wealth mindset as it keeps you focused and centered in the present moment.

   Practicing mindfulness is something I strive to do daily. I take a few minutes each day to focus on my breath and the present moment, which helps me clear my mind and stay focused on what's important. Furthermore, mindfulness keeps me calm and centered when faced with difficulties or obstacles.

7. Take Action: Finally, taking action is an essential element of cultivating a wealth mindset. It isn't enough to simply think positively and visualize your goals; you must also take steps toward achieving them.

   In taking action, I break my goals down into smaller, achievable tasks that can be completed each day. Each morning, I create a to-do list and prioritize those items that will bring me closer to achieving my objectives. By taking action every day, I stay motivated toward these goals and make progress toward them.

Cultivating a wealth mindset is an effective way to achieve abundance and success in all aspects of life. By adopting positive, abundance-focused thinking, we can overcome limiting beliefs and stay motivated toward reaching our objectives. Practical exercises such as recognizing limiting beliefs, practicing gratitude, creating vision boards, doing visualization exercises, using positive affirmations, practicing mindfulness exercises, and taking action all contribute toward developing this mindset. By integrating these exercises into daily living, you can cultivate this wealth mindset and be well on the path to a life of abundance and success.

Mastering the Mindset: Turn Limiting Beliefs into Abundance

This chapter serves as a holistic guide, offering a broader perspective on the intrinsic connection between mindset and prosperity. It lays the groundwork for financial triumph but also personal and spiritual growth, revealing how the right mindset can be your beacon guiding you to an abundant life. Its engaging exercises and useful tips are designed to help you nurture an abundance-oriented outlook. These are the tools and techniques you can wield on your journey to achieving both personal and financial prosperity.

Below are several questions to support you on your walk toward abundance and success. By thinking through these eight questions, you can gain better insight into the wealth mindset and its significance for success and abundance. Then by using the tips and practical exercises in this chapter, you will develop a wealth mindset enabling you to focus on your objectives, conquer obstacles and challenges, and remain motivated throughout your journey.

1. What is the distinction between a wealth mindset and a scarcity mindset? How do these affect your approach to achieving success and abundance?

2. What are some common limiting beliefs that could be keeping you from reaching your objectives? How can you identify and address them?

3. How can practicing gratitude help you cultivate a wealth mindset? What are some practical ways to incorporate it into your daily life?

4. Creating a vision board can keep you motivated and focused on your goals; what are some effective methods for creating one?

5. How does visualization aid you in cultivating a wealth mindset? How can you incorporate visualization into your daily routine?

6. What positive affirmations can help reprogram your subconscious mind and keep you focused on your goals? How can these be implemented into your routine?

7. How does mindfulness assist you in cultivating a wealth mindset? What are some practical ways that you can incorporate mindfulness into your daily life?

8. How can you cultivate a wealth mindset by surrounding yourself with positive people and environments? What are some effective methods for limiting your exposure to negativity and toxic influences?

CHAPTER II

HABITS OF SUCCESSFUL PEOPLE

This chapter swings open the door to an intriguing universe — a realm inhabited by successful individuals, where their secret recipes for accomplishment are unmasked. It transforms you into an archaeologist, unearthing the treasures of successful habits that can propel you toward your full potential. This deep dive into the world of successful individuals offers you a golden ticket, inviting you to join their ranks.

Success, contrary to popular belief, is not a chance gift bestowed by Lady Luck. Rather, it is the child of conscious dedication, perseverance, and the meticulous cultivation of advantageous habits. This chapter underscores that the path to success is no wild goose chase; it's a well-trodden road peppered with specific habits that, when adopted, can escalate life from mediocrity to unparalleled success.

Common Habits Shared by Successful People

The shared practices of successful people act like unique strands that, when woven together, create an incredibly robust safety net capable of catching you as you leap toward your goals. Each of these habits acts as a stepping stone that can facilitate a smooth journey across the river of life, leading to the shores of success and abundance.

Whether it's the discipline of a daily routine, the unwavering optimism in the face of adversity, or the resilience to bounce back after a setback, this chapter illuminates these practices in a manner that's both relatable and inspiring. By comprehending and incorporating these habits into your own life, you create a robust platform that supports your climb toward the summit of success.

Goal Setting: Successful people set clear and specific objectives for themselves. They know what they want to accomplish and have a strategy on how to get there. By setting objectives, they create an action plan for success and remain motivated to achieve them.

Time Management: Time is a valuable resource, and successful people know how to manage it effectively. They prioritize their tasks and focus on what matters most. Furthermore, they know when to delegate tasks and when to avoid distractions.

Lifelong Learning: Successful people embrace lifelong learning. They continuously seek out new knowledge and skills, constantly striving to improve themselves. They recognize that education is essential for growth and development as well as staying competitive in today's fast-paced world.

Positive Mindset: Successful people possess an upbeat, abundance-focused outlook. They believe in themselves and their abilities, staying focused on their objectives. Moreover, they feel grateful for all of life's blessings.

Persistence: Successful people demonstrate perseverance and resilience when faced with difficulties. They understand that setbacks are part of the journey to success, and they must keep going even when things get difficult.

Self-Care: Successful people place a priority on their physical, emotional, and mental well-being. They make time for exercise, nutritious eating, and healthy activities. In addition, they prioritize rest and relaxation as essential for keeping energy levels up while remaining focused.

Networking: Successful people understand the significance of building relationships and networking. They actively search out ways to connect with others in their field and cultivate strong connections with colleagues, mentors, and peers.

Accountability: Successful people take responsibility for their actions and results. They accept responsibility for errors made, learn from them, and seek out feedback that encourages constructive criticism.

Openness to Feedback and Criticism: Effective people actively seek feedback in order to improve themselves and reach success faster.

Incorporating these habits into our daily lives can lead to success and abundance in all areas of our lives. Doing so requires intentionality and a dedication to personal growth and development, but the rewards are worth all the effort.

Jim Rohn, the late motivational speaker and author, once said, "Success is neither magical nor mysterious. It is simply the natural outcome of consistently applying sound fundamentals."

To fully comprehend and adopt these habits, let's take a closer look at each one and discover how to best implement them on a daily basis.

Mastering the Nine Habits for Success

1. Setting Goals: Establishing goals is one of the most crucial habits of successful individuals. Without goals, we lack direction and purpose. Setting goals provides tangible targets to aim for,

infusing our lives with motivation and intention. With clear goals in place, mapping out new ones becomes much simpler — goals act as our personal road maps!

Crafting effective goals means they should be specific, measurable, and time-bound. This requires outlining your desired outcome, creating clear measures for success, and setting a deadline to reach these targets. In addition, breaking down larger tasks into more manageable steps introduces bite-size pieces that are easier to conquer.

Remember, setting goals is not just about big, grand targets. It's about creating a clear pathway of smaller, achievable targets that lead to your ultimate objective.

2. Time Management: This time-honored practice is an essential skill for success. Time management involves prioritizing tasks, avoiding distractions, and making the most of our time. One effective way to manage time effectively is creating a schedule or to-do list for each day. Doing so makes it easier to prioritize tasks and focus on what's most important. Furthermore, blocking out specific times for certain tasks helps prevent multitasking, which may decrease productivity levels.

Another key element of time management is learning how to ignore distractions. This could involve turning off notifications on your devices, avoiding time-wasting activities, and delegating tasks when possible. By managing time effectively, you can increase productivity levels and achieve more in less time.

3. Ongoing Learning: Successful individuals strive for lifelong learning, which involves seeking out new knowledge and skills as well as staying informed on the latest trends and developments in their industry. Furthermore, they remain open to feedback and constructive criticism when needed.

One way to foster the habit of continuous learning is reading regularly. This could include books, articles, and other materials related to your field or interests. Attending conferences, seminars, and other educational events also helps. By constantly improving yourself through knowledge acquisition, you will remain competitive and achieve greater success in the long run.

4. Positive Mindset: Fostering a positive and abundance-focused mindset is paramount for success. This requires cultivating gratitude for the blessings in our lives as well as believing in ourselves and our abilities.

   One effective way to cultivate a positive mindset is practicing gratitude daily. This can include taking time each day to reflect on what you are thankful for and expressing appreciation to others. In addition, focus on strengths and accomplishments instead of dwelling on shortcomings or failures.

   Another essential aspect of developing a positive mindset is setting realistic expectations and staying focused on those objectives. This requires accepting that setbacks and difficulties will occur while also believing in your capacity to overcome them and reach success.

5. Persistence: Success comes from being resilient in the face of challenges and obstacles. This requires taking risks, accepting failure, as well as maintaining a sense of determination and perseverance.

   One way to foster persistence is by developing a growth mindset. This involves viewing failures and setbacks as opportunities for development and learning rather than signs of inadequacy or incompetence. It also means staying focused on long-term objectives despite any short-term setbacks.

6. Self-Care Practice: Making our own physical, emotional, and mental well-being a priority is a critical factor in achieving success. This requires making time for exercise, healthy eating, and wellness activities such as massage, as well as prioritizing rest and relaxation.

The ideal way to cultivate healthy habits is by making them part of your daily schedule. This could include setting aside time for exercise and meal preparation, as well as practicing mindfulness and relaxation techniques. Also, setting realistic expectations helps you avoid overworking or neglecting physical and emotional needs.

7. Networking: Cultivating strong relationships and networking is essential for success. This involves seeking out opportunities to connect with others in your field and creating mutually beneficial connections with colleagues, mentors, and peers.

   One effective way to develop networking skills is by attending professional events and conferences. Staying connected with colleagues and peers through social media and other channels also pays dividends. By cultivating strong relationships and networking, you can open doors for yourself and boost your chances for success.

8. Accountability: Being accountable for our actions and outcomes is key to success. This requires accepting responsibility for our mistakes, learning from them, and taking steps to correct them.

   Setting clear objectives and establishing success criteria can foster accountability, helping you track your progress and see where improvements need to be made. A supportive network of colleagues, mentors, and peers can also hold you accountable, encouraging you to follow through with your commitments and responsibilities.

   Remember, taking ownership of your actions and outcomes allows you to learn, grow, and ultimately achieve greater success.

9. Openness to Feedback and Criticism: Success often involves a willingness to listen, learn, and adjust course based on feedback and criticism. This is not always easy, as it can be challenging to hear others' perspectives on our work or performance.

However, constructive criticism and feedback are invaluable tools for personal and professional growth. Let them help you identify your hidden areas or blind spots, enhance your strengths, and work on your weaknesses. By embracing feedback and criticism, you can refine your strategies, improve your skills, and accelerate your journey toward success.

These nine habits of successful people provide a proven road map for achieving success and abundance. Brian Tracy, an entrepreneur and author, once said that successful people possess successful habits. But it's not because they possess some secret formula or magic bullet. Creating these habits requires intentionality, consistent application, and dedication to personal development. They are not isolated events but an ongoing process of improvement and refinement, consistently reflecting on your behaviors and making necessary adjustments.

By setting clear and specific goals; managing time efficiently; constantly learning; maintaining a positive mindset; persevering when faced with difficulties; prioritizing health and wellness; building strong relationships and networking interactions, groups, and associations; as well as holding yourself accountable and being open to criticism and feedback, you, too, can master the habits that lead to the life of your dreams.

How to recognize and adopt these habits as your own

This section progresses from simply spotlighting the habits of successful individuals to guiding you on a deeper journey of self-analysis and transformation. It provides actionable insights for not only identifying but also incorporating these success-fostering habits into your daily life.

Adopting the routines and habits of triumphant individuals might initially seem like an uphill task, akin to wearing someone else's shoes. However, with unwavering determination, conscious effort, and a commitment to personal growth, it's absolutely possible to mold these habits into your own life, giving you a proven formula for success and abundance.

How do we recognize these habits, you might ask? Imagine being handed a pair of glasses that enable you to perceive the world in the way successful people do. This section serves as that special lens, offering clear explanations that allow you to discern the nuanced habits that define successful people.

Once identified, how do we adopt these habits? The answer lies in this section's practical tips and insightful guidelines. Like an experienced coach, it lays out a detailed training regimen, facilitating a seamless transition from merely acknowledging these habits to living them.

Ultimately, it equips you with the tools to weave these habits into the fabric of your daily life, thereby elevating your journey toward success and prosperity across all facets of life. As you'll discover, it becomes increasingly clear that anyone can walk in the footsteps of successful people when guided by the same habits, thereby unlocking their potential and stepping into a realm of limitless abundance. Here are some tips for identifying and adopting these habits.

Making the Habits Your Own

1. Examine Your Own Habits: Before establishing new habits, take an honest assessment of your existing habits. This means examining your daily routines and behaviors to identify areas for improvement — including time management, goal setting, continuous learning, mindset, persistence, health and wellness practices, networking, and accountability.

2. Define Specific Goals for Yourself: After identifying improvement areas, set specific and achievable objectives. This means outlining exactly what success looks like and creating metrics to measure that success. In addition, breaking down larger objectives into smaller, more manageable tasks will make progress much smoother.

3. Create a Plan: Once you set goals devising an action plan to reach them is essential. This involves identifying the habits you must develop and outlining steps you will take to incorporate them into your daily routine. Setting a timeline for completing your objectives and tracking progress along the way may be beneficial at this stage.

4. Enlist the Help of Role Models: Seeking out role models is one effective way to learn from successful people and adopt their habits. This could include mentors, colleagues, or others in your field who have achieved success and can serve as sources of motivation and advice. By observing their behaviors and drawing upon their experiences, you can gain invaluable insights on how to implement these practices in your own life.

5. Be Open to Change: Adopting new habits can be daunting, often necessitating us to step outside our comfort zones. To be open to change and embrace its discomfort, you must be willing to take risks, fail, and learn from mistakes. This requires being willing to try new things and embrace discomfort as part of growing as an individual.

6. Practice Consistency: Forming new habits requires time and dedication. It's essential to practice these behaviors consistently, even when they feel uncomfortable or difficult. By making them part of our daily routines, we can form new patterns of behavior and permanently integrate them into our lives.

7. Stay Accountable: Becoming accountable for our actions and outcomes is essential if we want to form new habits. This requires tracking progress, seeking feedback, and being open to constructive criticism. Moreover, having a support network of colleagues, mentors, and peers who can offer guidance and hold you accountable can be extremely helpful.

Michael Jordan's success can serve as an inspiring example of how powerful adopting successful habits can be. Not only was he one of basketball's all-time greats, but his success also stems from his commitment to developing positive habits.

Jordan was renowned for his intense focus and work ethic. He would arrive at the gym early and stay late, putting in countless hours of practice and conditioning. In addition, Jordan prioritized both his physical and mental well-being by following an intensive exercise and nutrition schedule as well as seeking out opportunities to learn and grow.

Jordan's dedication to these habits paid off handsomely throughout his career. He earned six NBA championships, five MVP awards, and numerous other accolades. But more than that, he became a role model to millions around the globe by modeling how important it is to cultivate positive habits and dedicate yourself to personal growth and development.

Kobe Bryant's career and life offer an equally inspiring testament to the power of successful habits. Known for his relentless "Mamba Mentality," Bryant's approach to his craft echoes the example set by Michael Jordan and beautifully demonstrates how the imitation of successful individuals can foster our own success. Kobe Bryant had an unparalleled dedication to his craft. He was known to arise at 4 a.m. to start his workouts, a habit he maintained consistently throughout his career. Like Jordan, Bryant was often the first player to arrive at the gym and the last one to leave, putting in more hours than most other players.

Bryant also mirrored Jordan's focus on both physical and mental fitness. His demanding workout routines and disciplined diet contributed to his physical readiness, while his dedication to studying game film and honing his mental toughness helped ensure his psychological edge. He constantly sought to learn and grow, whether that meant refining his skills or expanding his understanding of the game.

Bryant's adoption of these habits resulted in a storied career that spanned two decades, earning him five NBA championships, two Olympic gold medals, and four All-Star Game MVP awards, among other accolades. However, his influence extended beyond the basketball court. Bryant's "Mamba Mentality" — his relentless pursuit of greatness, unwavering focus, and refusal to be outworked — has inspired millions around the world.

This dedication to growth and excellence that Bryant adopted from Jordan showcases how imitating the habits of successful individuals can lead to personal success. It may require considerable time and effort, but through persistent application and a commitment to growth, we can realize our goals and unleash our full potential. Just as Bryant found his path to success by emulating Jordan, we, too, can achieve our own version of success by adopting the habits of those we admire.

Simply put, harnessing the habits of successful people is essential for achieving success and abundance in our own lives. By reflecting on our existing behaviors, setting clear objectives, creating a plan, finding role models who inspire us, being open to change, practicing consistency and staying accountable, we can adopt these habits and reach our full potential. As Michael Jordan famously said, "Failure is part of life — that's why I succeed." By accepting failure and learning from your mistakes, you, too, can cultivate the habits necessary for success while realizing your wildest dreams.

The Art of Breaking Bad Habits and Forming Beneficial Ones

In this section, we take a transformative turn as we delve into the art and science of habit alteration. It underscores that journeying toward success and abundance is not solely about collecting new positive habits. It's equally about discarding the old, detrimental ones, much like shedding an outdated version as we make way for a more empowered version of ourselves.

Breaking bad habits can feel like trying to dismantle a mountain with a spoon. It's a strenuous process that seems to stretch on forever. This section, however, hands you the proper equipment, revealing practical techniques that can ease this task, transforming it from an insurmountable challenge into an achievable goal.

At the same time, this section emphasizes the importance of forming beneficial habits. Like planting seeds in a garden, this process requires patience, consistent effort, and nurturing. It goes beyond just outlining the importance of such habits and actually teaches you how to sow and tend to these seeds of success.

Through an array of techniques ranging from how to manage triggers to bad habits, to creating an environment that fosters positive habits, this section serves as a manual for self-improvement. It acknowledges the investment of time and energy needed for such transformation but also ensures that the resulting success and abundance will be well worth the effort. And so you will transition from taking a possibly passive approach to personal growth to being an active participant, by accepting this invitation to engage in the dynamic process of habit transformation. Here are some techniques to foster the habit transformation process.

Seven Techniques for Habit Transformation

1. Recognize the Root Cause: The initial step in breaking a bad habit is to identify its underlying cause. This involves reflecting on why you do something and understanding what triggers it. For instance, if procrastinating is your habit, identify what triggers it and address those underlying issues.

2. Replace Negative Habits with Positive Ones: It's essential not only to replace the habit with a more positive one, but also to address the underlying issue that led to the development of the bad habit. This dual approach allows for a more comprehensive and enduring solution. By understanding and addressing the root cause, you are less likely to fall back into the same or similar negative habits, while the positive habit you cultivate in its place promotes better results. This means finding an alternative behavior that can serve as a healthier substitute for your negative one. For instance, if stress leads you to overeat, find healthier ways of managing stress such as exercise or meditation.

3. Practice Mindfulness: Mindfulness is the practice of being fully present in the moment and aware of our thoughts and behaviors. By practicing mindfulness, you can become more conscious of bad habits and make an intentional effort to replace them with positive ones. This requires paying attention to thoughts and behaviors as well as making deliberate choices about your actions.

4. Create an Action Plan: Crafting an action plan can be helpful when breaking bad habits and developing positive ones. This involves outlining specific steps you will take to replace negative behaviors with beneficial ones. For instance, if you want to stop procrastinating, create a schedule and commit to completing tasks within certain time frames.

5. Find Support: Breaking bad habits and developing positive ones can be daunting, so sometimes we need the assistance of others. This could include friends, family, colleagues, or a professional coach who can offer encouragement and hold you accountable.

6. Nurture Self-Care: Building positive habits requires a significant commitment of time and energy. So it's essential to prioritize your physical and mental well-being, get enough rest, and take breaks when needed. By practicing self-care, you can maintain the focus needed to create lasting change in your life.

7. Celebrate Small Wins: Fostering positive habits takes time, so it's essential to recognize and celebrate small victories along the way. By acknowledging progress, no matter how insignificant it may appear at first glance, you can more easily keep motivated and driven toward reaching larger objectives.

An inspiring example of the power of breaking bad habits and developing positive ones comes from Oprah Winfrey, widely renowned as one of the world's most successful and influential women. Winfrey's success was due not just to her natural talents but also to her commitment to cultivating beneficial practices.

Winfrey has faced many hardships throughout her life, such as poverty, abuse, and discrimination. Yet she refused to let these obstacles define her; instead, she focused on creating positive habits that would propel her toward success. She developed a commitment to continuous learning and personal growth, reading books, attending seminars, and seeking out mentors who could guide her along the way. Additionally, Winfrey practiced mindfulness and self-care by making time for exercise, meditation, and relaxation.

Winfrey's habits paid off handsomely: she achieved great success as both a media mogul and philanthropist, amassing an estimated net worth of over $2.6 billion. As founder of Oprah Winfrey Network (OWN), one of television's most successful networks ever, she has also been recognized as one of the world's most powerful women, having received numerous awards for her contributions in entertainment, philanthropy, and social justice.

Winfrey's success is a testament to the power of breaking bad habits and developing positive ones. She refused to let her past define her. She focused instead on creating habits that would lead her toward success. By dedicating herself to personal growth and development, practicing mindfulness, practicing self-care, and seeking out support from others, Winfrey was able to overcome all odds and realize her most ambitious aspirations.

Changing bad habits and developing positive ones is a key step to achieving success. By recognizing the root cause of negative behaviors, replacing them with positive ones, practicing mindfulness, creating an action plan, seeking support, practicing self-care, and celebrating small wins, you, too, can form the habits necessary for success — just like Oprah Winfrey has demonstrated through her inspirational example!

Practical Exercises for Adopting Successful Habits

In this part of *The Wealth Spark*, the focus shifts from theory to hands-on application. This section is like a well-equipped gym. It's designed not just to expose you to the idea of beneficial habits but to actively engage you in a set of practical exercises to help you infuse these traits into your daily life.

Adopting successful habits might seem like trying to fly a kite in a gusty wind — challenging and unpredictable. However, these habits act as the indispensable pillars supporting the greater structure of success and abundance. Mastering them is paramount for anyone who aims to excel in every aspect of life.

Use this section as a personal trainer offering a diverse range of practical exercises tailored to help you internalize these successful habits. It's like a "do-it-yourself" kit for self-improvement, encouraging you to roll up your sleeves and immerse yourself in the process of habit transformation.

But the assistance doesn't stop there. In addition to these exercises, this section provides actionable tips to ease the transition, much like training wheels on a bicycle. These tips serve as your navigational beacon, guiding you through the choppy waters of change toward the serene shores of success and abundance.

Think of this section as a launchpad, preparing you for your journey toward a prosperous life. By the end, you won't just understand the habits of successful people; you'll be equipped with the knowledge and tools to make them your own.

Nine Practical Exercises for Adopting Successful Habits

1. Define Your Goals: The first step in adopting successful habits is recognizing what you want to accomplish and setting achievable yet specific objectives. For instance, if you want to launch a business venture, then you need to determine the type of busi-

ness venture, how much money needs to be invested, and the steps needed in order to get going.

2. Define Your Why: Once you've identified your goals, it's essential to determine why. Ask yourself why you want to reach these objectives and what drives you. For instance, if starting a business is on your bucket list, your why could be financial freedom, having an impact on society, or creating a legacy for family members.

3. Create a Plan: Crafting an action plan can help you stay on track while developing successful habits. This involves outlining specific steps you will take to reach your objectives, both short and long term. For instance, in the business venture example, your steps might include researching your target market, creating a business plan, and finding funding sources.

4. Look for Role Models: Finding role models can be an effective tool in adopting successful habits. This involves recognizing people who have achieved similar objectives and studying their habits and behaviors. Again, in the business venture example, seek out successful entrepreneurs and study their business strategies and tactics.

5. Focus on One Habit at a Time: Adopting successful habits can be overwhelming, so it is essential to prioritize one at a time. This means identifying an action item that will help you reach your objectives and making a commitment to practicing it regularly. In the business venture example, developing the habit of networking by attending business social events and building relationships with other entrepreneurs might be highly beneficial.

6. Practice Consistency: When developing successful habits, consistency is key. This requires making a commitment to practice your chosen habit consistently, even when it is difficult or inconvenient. If a successful entrepreneurial venture is your objective, then it would make sense to allocate some time each week for business development activities.

7. Stay Accountable: Accountability is paramount when developing successful habits. This may involve finding support from others who can hold you accountable and offer motivation along the way. For the business example, joining a business networking group, hiring an accountability coach, or finding someone who shares your goals and can help keep you on track are all great options for accountability.

8. Harness the Power of a Morning Routine: Starting your day off on the right foot with a morning ritual can set the tone for success throughout the day. Use these tips for creating an effective morning routine:

   Set an Alarm Clock for the Same Time Every Day: Clock in at a consistent wake-up time to help regulate your internal body clock and promote better sleep quality.

   Greet the Day with Water: Drink a glass of water as you begin your day, to help hydrate your body and aid digestion.

   Practice Gratitude: Take a few moments each morning to reflect on what you are thankful for, which can help shift your perspective toward positivity and abundance.

   Move Your Body: Involve yourself in some form of physical activity, such as stretching or doing a short workout, to invigorate your body and improve focus.

   Set Intentions: Take a few moments to set intentions for the day. This involves identifying key tasks or goals you want to achieve and visualizing yourself completing them.

   Minimize Distractions: Try to limit distractions during your morning routine by turning off notifications on your phone and avoiding social media platforms.

   Strive for Consistency: Make it a priority to stick with your morning routine even when it is difficult or inconvenient. Consistency is the key to building successful habits.

9. Become a Master at Time-Blocking: This practical exercise involves setting aside specific blocks of time for various tasks and activities. Here are some tips for successfully practicing time-blocking:

   Define Your Priorities: Prioritize the most essential tasks or activities to be accomplished each day and dedicate time for them first.

   Break Tasks into Smaller Components: Unbundle larger tasks into more manageable, bite-sized chunks, and set aside time for each one.

   Utilize a Calendar or Planner: Use a calendar, planner, or other scheduling tool to plan out time blocks and keep track of commitments.

   Minimize Distractions: Avoid interruptions during your time blocks by turning off notifications and avoiding social media.

   Take Breaks: Be sure to take breaks as needed between time blocks to rest and recharge.

   Regularly Evaluate and Adjust: Periodically assess your time-blocking system to optimize efficiency and effectiveness.

Elon Musk, the innovative entrepreneur and founder of companies like SpaceX and Tesla, exemplifies the principles of adopting success habits. Known for his visionary thinking and unflinching dedication, Musk embodies a tangible blueprint of successful habits in action.

Firstly, Musk is renowned for setting ambitious goals — whether it's revolutionizing transportation with electric vehicles or aiming to colonize Mars. His goals always carry profound significance, highlighting the practice of "figuring out why they matter." For Musk, these goals are not just about personal success but about addressing major challenges facing humanity.

Secondly, Musk is meticulous about "creating a plan." His approach is underpinned by "First Principles Thinking," a problem-solving method that involves breaking down complex problems into their fundamental parts and then reconstructing solutions from the ground up. This approach allows him to formulate innovative strategies to realize his ambitious goals.

Thirdly, Musk has often spoken about his "role models," such as inventors like Thomas Edison and Nikola Tesla, showing that he also understands the importance of learning from those who have achieved success.

In terms of "focusing on one habit at a time," Musk is known for his single-eyed focus when he's working on a project, demonstrating the power of single-tasking and concentration.

Musk's "consistency" is legendary. Despite myriad challenges, he has never wavered in pursuit of his goals, demonstrating an unwavering commitment to his vision.

In terms of "staying accountable," Musk stands out for his candor in admitting mistakes and taking responsibility for them. This reflects a willingness to learn from failures, a habit that is crucial for long-term success.

Finally, Musk's infamous work schedule, including his structured time blocks, reflects the "practical exercises" recommended in *The Wealth Spark*. For instance, Musk breaks his schedule into five-minute slots and maintains a rigorous morning routine, demonstrating a highly disciplined approach to time management.

Elon Musk's habits illustrate how adopting the practices outlined in this chapter can drive remarkable success and abundance. By learning from his example and following this section's practical exercises and tips, you can cultivate similar habits that will propel you toward your goals and allow you to live your best life.

Adopting successful habits is essential for achieving an abundant life. By setting goals, figuring out why they matter, creating a plan, seeking out role models, focusing on one habit at a time, practicing consistency and staying accountable, you can cultivate the habits necessary for success. Along with daily practical exercises like developing a morning routine or time blocking, you'll be on your way to reaching those milestones and living the life you desire.

Strategies for Success Habit Creation

At this point in the journey, the focus intensifies on adopting successful habits as a means to achieve abundance and success. It's akin to a sculptor working on a piece of marble, with each chisel strike representing a habit and the finished statue signifying a successful and abundant life.

True success and abundance are far from accidental. They are the byproducts of an intricate mosaic of habits that successful individuals practice daily. This part of the chapter acts as your tour guide, leading you through the labyrinth of these behaviors, unveiling the secret pathways to prosperity.

This chapter is not just a theoretical discussion; it serves as a tool kit, equipping you with practical strategies for grafting these habits onto your tree of life. This is where all of the knowledge already presented in the chapter turns into action.

Understanding the shared habits of successful individuals is the first step in this habit transformation process. The chapter then moves on to replacing the negative weeds in your habit garden with positive flowers, dramatically altering the landscape of your life.

The chapter further arms you with exercises and tips not just to adopt but to live and breathe these successful habits, transforming them from foreign concepts into second nature. This not only sets the stage for achieving success but also acts as a catalyst helping you reach your goals with enhanced speed and efficiency.

In essence, this part of *The Wealth Spark* is like a masterclass, with successful individuals as your tutors. It provides an insightful blueprint enabling you to emulate their habits, fast-track your progress, and ultimately step into a realm of boundless success and abundance. Therefore, by understanding common habits shared by successful people, replacing negative habits with positive ones, and putting the exercises and tips into practice, you can set yourself up for success and reach your goals more quickly.

Use the questions below as a framework for reflecting on your own habits and behaviors, and for identifying areas for growth and improvement. Put the chapter's tools and strategies to work for you as you actively engage with these questions. As a result, you'll gain greater appreciation for the importance of developing successful habits, deeper insight into what habits lead to success, and the resolve to begin implementing them in your own life to ignite your full potential.

1. What habits do successful individuals share, and how can you incorporate these practices into your own life?

2. How can you identify the habits that are holding you back and replace them with positive, productive routines?

3. What are some practical techniques for breaking bad habits and creating positive ones?

4. How can you create a strategy to form successful habits and hold yourself accountable for your progress?

5. How can you harness the power of consistency to make successful habits part of your everyday routine?

6. What are some practical steps you can take to create successful habits, such as developing a morning ritual or practicing time blocking?

7. How can you identify role models and learn from their successful habits and behaviors?

8. What challenges may arise as you strive to form successful habits, and how can you overcome them in order to reach your goals?

CHAPTER III

THE POWER OF VISUALIZATION AND AFFIRMATIONS

This chapter reveals a realm of internal resources that, when harnessed correctly, can prove transformative in attracting abundance and success. Imagine having the power to shape your reality through your thoughts and words, much like a potter molding clay. This is the remarkable potential of visualization and affirmations.

Visualization is akin to a mental rehearsal or "mind movie" of your aspirations. It enables you to experience your dreams and goals in your mind's eye even before they materialize. This section serves as your guide to understanding the power of visualization. It illustrates how this simple yet potent technique can effectively engage your subconscious mind and thereby make your objectives seem more achievable.

Similarly, affirmations act like seeds sown in the fertile soil of your subconscious mind. These positive, present-tense statements can alter your thought patterns, replacing limiting beliefs with empowering convictions. As you navigate this chapter, you'll gain a deeper understanding of how affirmations work to function as a catalyst for personal transformation and success.

The Role of Visualization and Affirmations in Manifestation

Notably, the section also underscores how these two tools, when used in conjunction, can be highly potent. Like the two wings of a bird, visualization and affirmations can work in harmony to lift you to greater heights of success and abundance.

Through theory combined with practical examples, this section makes clear how to effectively harness the power of these techniques to align your thoughts and actions with your aspirations. The journey it offers is magical, transforming you from a passive dreamer into an active creator of your destiny.

In essence, this section on visualization and affirmations invites you to tap into the immense power of your mind, using these two powerful tools for manifesting your dreams and igniting your path to prosperity.

What Is Visualization?

Visualization is the practice of using your imagination to form an inner vision of something you wish to achieve or experience. It involves conjuring up a vivid mental picture of what you wish to manifest and drawing upon all senses to bring this image alive.

Visualization works by tapping into your subconscious mind's power of creating a mental image in vivid detail. Doing so activates the reticular activating system (RAS) in your brain. By focusing your attention on what matters most, it helps you identify opportunities and take actions that move you toward reaching your goals.

Visualization has been used for millennia as a powerful success manifestation tool—from ancient spiritual practices to contemporary self-help books. Visualization has long been recognized as an effective technique for achieving goals and aspirations.

Five Tips for Effective Visualization

Follow these steps to maximize the impact of visualization:

1. Define Your Goals and Objectives: Before beginning visualization, identify what you hope to bring into manifestation in your life. This could be a specific goal like starting your own business, attracting the perfect mate, or having an overall feeling such as happiness, peace, or fulfillment.

2. Create a Detailed Image: Once you've identified what you want, create an accurate mental representation in your mind, using all five senses to make the image as vivid and real as possible.

3. Focus on the Feeling: As you visualize your desired outcome, pay attention to the feelings associated with it. Imagine what it would feel like to reach your goal or experience what you desire.

4. Repeat Regularly: To solidify the image in your mind and activate the RAS, it's essential to repeat visualization daily. Carve out time each day to fully visualize your desired outcome.

5. Take Action: Visualization alone won't bring about your desired outcomes. It's essential that you take steps toward reaching those goals, using visualization as a motivating tool to stay focused along the way.

What Are Affirmations?

Affirmations are positive statements we repeat to ourselves to reinforce positive beliefs and attitudes. They serve to replace negative self-talk or limiting thoughts with more empowering and upbeat ones.

Affirmations work by tapping into the subconscious mind to alter beliefs and attitudes. When you repeat affirmations frequently, they become part of you — by altering thoughts and behaviors as you internalize their positive message.

For decades, affirmations have been used as a powerful tool for personal growth and self-improvement. In self-help books and from motivational speakers, affirmations have become widely recognized as an effective method for life enhancement.

Five Tips for Effective Affirmations

Follow these steps for effective use of affirmations:

1. Recognize Limiting Beliefs: Before using affirmations, identify any limiting beliefs that are holding you back. These could include negative self-talk, self-doubt, or feelings that you're not good enough. Once your limiting beliefs have been identified, affirmations can help provide hope and motivation in times of struggle.

2. Create Positive Affirmations: For each of your limiting beliefs, create affirmations to counter them. These should be short, affirming statements that speak to your worth and potential. For example, if you have a limiting belief like "I am not good enough to succeed," you could create a positive affirmation such as "I am capable and deserving of success." Or, if you often think, "I can't handle the challenges that come my way," counter that with an affirmation like "I am resilient and can handle whatever comes my way."

3. Reinforce Frequently: To most effectively internalize the positive messages, repeat your affirmations frequently. Say them aloud or write them down so that the reinforcement becomes part of your daily routine.

4. Believe in Affirmations: For affirmations to be truly helpful, you must believe that they are true and that you are capable of

reaching your objectives. Have faith that these words of encouragement are true. Trust that these positive messages that came from within or through you from your higher power, reflect who you truly are and can help guide your decisions.

5. Take Action: Affirmations alone won't get you where you want to go. Take action toward manifesting your goals! Affirmations have the power of manifestation, so use them as tools for staying motivated and focused!

Five Tips for Maximizing the Power of Visualization and Affirmations

Visualization and affirmations are powerful tools in themselves, but there are ways to maximize their effectiveness. Try these tips for getting the most out of these techniques:

1. Repetition Is Key: Do them regularly for maximum impact! Carve out time each day to visualize your goals and repeat positive affirmations.

2. Utilize Emotion: When visualizing and using affirmations, draw from the emotions associated with your desired outcome. Doing so helps reinforce the positive message and fosters a feeling of motivation and excitement.

3. Be Specific: When visualizing, be as specific as possible about what you wish to create. Doing this helps focus your mind and activates or signals the reticular activating system (RAS).

4. Use Present-Tense Affirmations: When crafting affirmations, use the present tense to convey that your desired outcome has already taken place. For example, instead of saying "I will become a successful entrepreneur," affirm "I am a successful entrepreneur." The former implies a future event, while the latter makes it present and more real in your mind.

5. Have Faith in Yourself: For visualization and affirmations to be effective, you must have faith in yourself and your abilities. Believe in yourself and your ability to achieve your objectives while remaining upbeat and optimistic.

An Inspiring Story: Jim Carrey's Visualization Technique

Jim Carrey is a renowned actor and comedian best known for his roles in films like *The Mask* and *Ace Ventura: Pet Detective*. But before becoming an accomplished Hollywood star, Jim was just another struggling actor attempting to break into the industry.

Carrey used visualization to stay motivated and focused, writing himself a check for $10 million that had been post-dated to Thanksgiving 1995. He carried the check with him everywhere he went and imagined himself receiving it as part of an affirmation ritual.

Years later, Carrey earned a whopping $10 million paycheck for his role in *Dumb and Dumber*. Through visualization and faith in himself, he achieved his goal.

This story serves as a powerful reminder of the power of visualization and affirmations. By creating an intense image of his desired outcome and believing in his capacity for success, Carrey was able to manifest his goals and experience incredible success.

Visualization and affirmations are two powerful tools for manifesting abundance and success in your life. By consistently using these techniques, you can access the power of your subconscious mind and align your thoughts and actions with your desired outcomes.

In this section, we examined the concept of visualization and affirmations, how they work together, and how to utilize them efficiently to achieve goals. Also provided are tips for maximizing their power as well as an inspiring story to motivate you to try these techniques out for yourself.

Overall, visualization and affirmations are powerful tools for achieving goals and creating a successful life. Whether we aim for financial gain, improved relationships, or the pursuit of passions, visualization and affirmations can help us manifest our desires and lead us down a path of fulfillment and contentment. By altering your thoughts and beliefs, you'll reprogram your subconscious mind so that your actions align with the life you want.

Techniques for Visualization and Affirmation

Our journey begins in the depths of a grand library, rich with wisdom and knowledge from countless generations. This place we are exploring is no ordinary section; it's the mind's collection of tools and techniques for visualization and affirmation.

When we first step into the visualization chamber of this library, we encounter various volumes and scrolls, each representing a unique technique. Each one of these is a unique path through the labyrinth of the mind, a way to visualize our dreams and ambitions. It's like a paintbrush dipped in the vibrant hues of your imagination, ready to create a masterpiece on the canvas of your mind.

We'll study the mysteries of guided visualizations, a technique like an ancient cartographer's map guiding us to manifest our dreams into reality. Similarly, we'll grasp the power of vision boards, tools that turn our aspirations into tangible visual reminders, anchoring us firmly on our path toward success.

Next, we transition into the affirmation atrium of this grand library. Here, the shelves are lined with techniques that harness the power of positive self-talk, acting as our inner cheerleaders. Like a skilled composer tuning their instrument, these techniques help us fine-tune our thought patterns, turning dissonant notes of self-doubt into a harmonious symphony of self-belief.

Through methods like crafting custom affirmations and integrating affirmations into daily routines, we'll learn to sing our unique melody of success. Each technique is a key to unlocking the communication with our subconscious mind, rewriting the scripts that guide our lives.

This section is a grand adventure through the halls of wisdom, but it is not a one-way journey. It is an interactive exploration that allows us to adapt and modify what we find. The visualization and affirmation techniques presented here aren't fixed like stone tablets; instead, they are as flexible as clay, ready to be molded to fit our unique journeys toward abundance and success.

As we traverse through this labyrinth of knowledge, we're not just spectators; we are explorers charting our unique paths. With every technique we learn, we'll discover new ways to navigate our minds and manifest our dreams. Armed with this newfound wisdom, we are ready to step into the practical exercise arena, where we will put our learning into action, strengthening our grasp on these powerful tools.

Six Techniques for Affirming and Visualizing

1. Vision Board

A vision board is an effective visualization tool that involves creating a collage of images and words to represent your goals and aspirations. By looking at this board frequently, you can reinforce positive messages and stay focused on manifesting your vision.

Create a vision board by gathering images and words that represent your desired outcomes. You can search magazines, newspapers, or online sources for inspiring images and quotes that speak to you. Once collected, arrange the graphics on a poster board or bulletin board or other display so it's prominently visible.

2. Guided Visualization

Guided visualization involves listening to a guided meditation or visualization exercise. The idea behind guided visualization is to use suggestions to conjure up an intense mental image of your desired outcome.

To practice guided visualization, find a quiet and comfortable place to sit or lie down. Then listen to an audio guided meditation or visualization exercise that focuses you on your desired outcome. As you listen, try to form an accurate mental image of what you wish to manifest and feel the emotions associated with that vision.

3. Positive Self-Talk

Positive self-talk involves using affirmations and positive statements to instill an attitude of abundance and success into your subconscious mind. By consistently repeating these affirmations, you can reprogram your subconscious mind, altering how you view yourself and what potential lies within.

Practice positive self-talk by first recognizing negative patterns of thought that are holding you back. Then, create a list of affirmations and statements to counteract those negative ones; repeat these phrases frequently to reinforce the message and foster feelings of motivation and optimism.

4. Future Self-Visualization

Future self-visualization involves visualizing your future self and the life you wish to create. By creating an accurate mental image of this ideal future self, it becomes easier to align your thoughts and actions with goals; plus, it provides motivation and focus.

To practice future self-visualization, find a quiet and comfortable place to sit or lie down. Close your eyes and create an image of yourself living the life that you wish to manifest, experiencing all of the emotions associated with that reality.

5. Gratitude Practice

Gratitude is an invaluable tool in manifesting abundance and success. By focusing on what you are thankful for, you attract more positivity and wealth into your life.

Practice gratitude by creating a daily list of things you are thankful for. You can write them down in a journal or simply consider them mentally. By focusing on the positive aspects of your life, you will cultivate an attitude of gratitude and abundance.

6. Mirror Work

Mirror work involves looking in a mirror and repeating positive affirmations and statements to yourself. By looking into your own eyes, affirming your worth and your potential, you can cultivate self-love and confidence.

Mirror work is an effective tool for self-improvement. Find a quiet area and sit in front of a mirror, looking into your own eyes. Repeat positive affirmations and statements to yourself like "I am worthy of love and success" or "I can achieve my objectives."

Visualization and affirmation techniques are of maximum benefit only when they are incorporated into your daily routine. Here are some tips for making these practices part of your regimen:

Seven Tips for Integrating Visualization and Affirmation into Your Day

1. Make Time for Visualization and Affirmation

Set aside time in your daily schedule to practice visualization and affirmation. This could be as little as five minutes each day or up to an hour, depending on what works best for you and your lifestyle. By making this practice part of your routine, you are more likely to stick with it and reap its rewards in the long run.

2. Utilize Reminders

Set reminders for yourself to practice visualization and affirmation. This could be in the form of daily notifications on your phone or computer or by placing a visual cue such as a picture or quote in an easily visible place where you will encounter it frequently.

3. Practice Gratitude Daily

Incorporate gratitude into your daily routine by beginning each day with a gratitude practice such as journaling or reflecting on what you are thankful for. Gratitude can set the tone for an abundant and productive day by encouraging positive thought patterns.

4. Create a Vision Board

Construct a vision board to remind yourself of your goals and aspirations. Hang it up somewhere prominent, such as in your workspace or bedroom. Frequently viewing this visual reminder will help reinforce its encouraging message and keep you focused on your mission.

5. Utilize Positive Affirmations

Use positive affirmations regularly to reinforce the message of abundance and success. Counteract any negative self-talk or limiting beliefs with affirmations that focus on your strengths and potential.

6. Practice Guided Visualization

Add guided visualization to your daily routine by listening to a guided meditation or visualization exercise each day. Find a quiet and comfortable place to sit or lie down, then create a detailed mental image of the desired outcome.

7. Practice Mirror Work

Incorporate mirror work into your daily routine by looking in the mirror and repeating positive affirmations and statements to yourself. By affirming your worth and potential, you can build a sense of self-love and confidence.

By incorporating visualization and affirmation techniques into your daily routine, you can attract abundance and success into all areas of life. With regular practice and dedication, you can reprogram your subconscious mind with new beliefs about yourself and what potential you possess. As Tony Robbins once said, "Beliefs have the power to create or destroy; humans have the incredible capacity to take any experience they encounter and turn it into either something that dis-empowers them or something that literally saves their lives." Choose to empower yourself with positive beliefs so that you may create the life of abundance and success that you deserve.

Visualization and Affirmation: Practical Exercises

Imagine stepping into a personal training ground, where theory meets practice and knowledge transforms into action. This section serves as that training field for you, preparing you to engage with and master the techniques of visualization and affirmation in your daily life.

Picture yourself at the break of dawn, greeted by the first rays of the sun. This tranquil time becomes your sanctuary for a morning visual-ization routine. Here, you're not just passively picturing your dreams but actively shaping them, like a sculptor chiseling away to create a masterpiece. Each stroke of your visualization reveals more of your dreams and aspirations, turning the formless into something palpable.

As you go about your day, imagine the power of integrating affir-mations. They become your loyal companions, whispering words of encouragement in your ear, like a lifelong friend. From the hustle of your work hours to the tranquility of your evening wind-down, these positive assertions are always by your side, infusing your thoughts with positivity and strength.

Consider the versatility of creating a visualization journal. It's like having a magical book where you can scribe your dreams and aspi-rations. Each page is a new opportunity, a blank canvas waiting to be filled with the hues of your future success.

Similarly, envision keeping affirmation cards close to you. These little reminders become your mental boosters, ready to inspire and motivate you whenever needed. Like holding a compass in an unknown terrain, these affirmation cards keep you oriented toward your goal, no matter where you are.

By participating in these exercises, you are not merely practicing techniques but also learning to weave them into the tapestry of your life. You're adapting them, making them your own, and in the process, you're transforming into a maestro of manifestation.

By the end of this section, you'll have a repertoire of exercises uniquely tailored to you. You'll be an artisan of abundance, using the tools of visualization and affirmation to craft a remarkable journey to success.

Eight Practical Exercises for a Daily Visualization/Affirmation Practice

1. Morning Visualization

Kick off your day with a visualization exercise. Spend a few minutes each morning visualizing your goals and desired outcomes, creating a vivid mental image of what you hope to accomplish, then feeling the emotions associated with that success. By starting each day off on a positive note, you set the atmosphere for an effective and abundant day ahead.

2. Positive Affirmations

Use positive affirmations throughout the day to reinforce the message of abundance and success. Counteract negative self-talk or limiting beliefs with affirmations that focus on your strengths and potential. For instance, if you struggle with self-doubt, repeat affirmations such as "I am confident and capable" or "I trust in my abilities and believe in myself."

3. Visualization Journal

Create a visualization journal to keep yourself motivated toward reaching your goals and desired outcomes. Write down your objectives in the journal, along with visual representations of them. Spend a few minutes each day looking at this journal and visualizing what success looks like for you. Regular reflection helps reinforce positive messages and keeps your focus on reaching these objectives.

4. Guided Visualization

Incorporate guided visualization into your daily routine by listening to a guided meditation or visualization exercise each day. Find a quiet and comfortable place to sit or lie down, then create an image in your mind of the desired outcome. There are plenty of online resources for guided visualization exercises.

5. Gratitude Practice

Make gratitude part of your daily routine by taking a few minutes each day to reflect on what you are thankful for. Doing this can help shift your focus from lack and scarcity to abundance and gratitude. By focusing on the positive aspects of your life, you create an atmosphere of abundance and attract greater positivity.

6. Vision Board

Create a vision board to remind yourself of your goals and desires. Display the board in an accessible location where it will be seen often, such as your workspace or bedroom. By regularly viewing this positive reminder, you will stay motivated to reach those objectives.

7. Mirror Work

Make mirror work part of your daily routine by looking in the mirror and repeating positive affirmations and statements to yourself. Affirming your self-worth and potential will build self-love and confidence, helping transform negative self-talk or limiting beliefs. Mirror work can be an effective tool for changing negative thoughts about yourself that limit you.

8. Create Affirmation Cards

Keep affirmation cards on hand throughout the day. Write down positive affirmations and statements on small cards, then keep them with you in your pocket or wallet. Whenever you feel low or overwhelmed, pull out those affirmation cards and repeat them aloud to yourself.

Implementing visualization and affirmations on a daily basis takes practice and dedication. Making these practices part of your routine will reprogram your subconscious mind, altering your beliefs about yourself and what possibilities await you. With regular repetition and dedication, you will focus on manifesting the abundant life that you deserve

Transformative Tools for Achieving Abundance and Success

This chapter has shone a spotlight on the transformative tools of visualization and affirmation, igniting their potential to help shape your reality. It has served as a master key, opening the door to the powerful realm of your subconscious mind and enabling you to attract what you truly desire.

Going beyond superficial understanding, the chapter delved deeply into the mechanics of these techniques, illuminating how they forge a connection with your subconscious and thereby influence your reality. It paints a vivid picture of how you can sculpt your thoughts and words to shape your world, manifesting abundance and success.

The chapter also presented a gallery of visualization and affirmation strategies that successful individuals have utilized to reach their pinnacle. It gifted you a treasure trove of practical exercises and tips to seamlessly blend these practices into the rhythm of your everyday life. These insights are designed to harmonize your affirmations and visualizations with your core beliefs, dismantle mental barriers, and kindle a persistent spark of motivation.

Think of this chapter as your personal guidebook, an all-encompassing manual on harnessing the power of visualization and affirmation to magnetize and attract abundance and success in every facet of your life. By diligently and consistently implementing the outlined techniques and exercises, you're likely to experience enhanced clarity, focus, and drive toward achieving your goals and creating a life of prosperity and fulfillment.

The following thought-provoking questions are designed to help deepen your understanding and appreciation of the power of visualization and affirmation. Thoughtfully answering them will not only expand your awareness but also help you more effectively weave these potent tools into the fabric of your life and manifest your dreams.

1. How can visualization and affirmation help me reach my goals for abundance and success?

2. What are some common visualization and affirmation strategies employed by successful individuals?

3. How can I best incorporate visualization and affirmation practices into my daily routine?

4. How can I ensure that my affirmations and visualizations align with my core values and goals?

5. How can visualization and affirmation techniques help me overcome limiting beliefs and negative self-talk?

6. How can I measure the success of my visualization and affirmation practices?

7. How can I ensure consistency and motivation in those daily practices?

8. How can I overcome hesitation or doubt about these techniques and fully believe in their potential?

CHAPTER IV

ACTION: ATTAINING ABUNDANCE AND SUCCESS

The next leg of our journey through *The Wealth Spark* illuminates a crucial component of the wealth creation formula — ACTION. Much like a boat needs to be rowed to reach the shore, positive thinking and visualization must be paired with purposeful action to manifest our desires.

This chapter underscores the undeniable fact that dreaming about success and abundance is just the prologue of our wealth narrative. The ensuing sections hinge upon the choices we make, the steps we take, and the relentless pursuit of our goals. It is within action that dreams evolve from mere imaginings into tangible outcomes. Without action, even the most positive thoughts and the clearest visualizations are like an orchestra without a conductor — rich with potential but lacking direction.

The Importance of Taking Action

As we delve into the heart of this chapter, we explore the symbiotic relationship between positive thinking, visualization, and action. We discover how these elements interact to form a potent trifecta that sets the foundation for achieving success and abundance.

This chapter is also designed as a practical guide, offering actionable steps that you can readily incorporate into your daily life. Whether it's breaking down your larger goals into manageable tasks, developing a consistent routine, or maintaining an unwavering commitment to your objectives, these tips serve as a compass, guiding you on your journey toward abundance and success.

In essence, this chapter is akin to a personal coach who reminds you that abundance and success are not merely about the destination but also about the journey. It's the process of making conscious, consistent, and courageous choices every day, turning your dreams into reality, one action step at a time. Through this exploration, you'll come to appreciate the profound truth that your life's abundance and success lie in your own hands — or more precisely, in your actions.

In other words, to create abundance and success in our lives, it's not enough to just think positively or visualize our goals. We must also take action toward achieving them. Without action, even the best intentions and affirmations may remain unrealized.

Understanding the Power of Action: The Engine Behind Success

Life, in its richest form, is a dance between dreams and actions. We all harbor dreams, we all aspire, and within us, we carry a canvas painted with the colors of our deepest desires. But dreams alone, no matter how vibrant, do not manifest into reality without action. Action breathes life into these dreams, transmuting our aspirational canvas into a tangible masterpiece. In this sense, action serves as the engine that propels us toward success and abundance.

Imagine standing at the base of a mountain, with your goal at the summit, veiled by the mists of challenges and obstacles. The dreamer in you visualizes standing on that peak, savoring the victory and the exhilarating view. But to ascend to the summit, you need more than just the vision. You need to put one foot in front of the other, navigate the terrain, adjust your path as needed, and persevere in the climb, no matter how arduous. This is the power of action.

In the world of sailing, there's a saying: "You can't steer a stationary ship." Regardless of how well you know your destination, how expertly you've charted your course, or how accurately you've read the weather, without setting sail and making headway, you'll remain docked. Similarly, in life, no matter how compelling our goals or meticulous our plans, it's only through action that we can make progress, adjust our course as needed, and ultimately reach our destination.

Kathrine Switzer's story is a testament to the transformative power of action and the pursuit of one's dreams. In 1967, women were not allowed to officially participate in marathons. However, Kathrine, with a burning desire to prove that women were capable of running the distance, registered for the Boston Marathon using her initials, K. V. Switzer.

During the marathon, race official Jock Semple noticed Kathrine, realized she was a woman, and tried to forcefully remove her from the course. Unfazed by the opposition, Kathrine refused to back down and continued running. Her determination and resilience in the face of adversity made headlines around the world, sparking a movement for women's inclusion in marathons.

Kathrine Switzer's courage and willingness to take action paved the way for countless women to pursue their athletic aspirations. Her story serves as a powerful reminder that action, even in the face of resistance, can create meaningful change and break down barriers.

So, what gives action such power? The secret lies in its transformative capability. Action translates our inner world into outer reality. It's a language that the universe comprehends. It's the currency we exchange for success. Each action we take, no matter how seemingly small, leaves an imprint on the world. Each step, each decision, each movement reshapes our destiny, gradually molding it to align with our deepest aspirations.

As we embark on this journey of understanding the power of action, remember that it's action that separates the dreamers from the doers, the successful from the stagnant. Through action, we engage with the world, manifest our intentions, and create our desired reality. It's the bridge between the metaphysical world of thoughts and the physical world of results. Embrace it, and you unlock the door to abundance and success. Your dreams have provided you with the destination — let your actions command the ship. Let's set sail!

1. Self-Awareness: Recognize the Role of Action

The journey to harness the power of action begins with self-awareness. Recognize that your present circumstances, whether satisfying or lacking, have been shaped by your past actions or inactions. Your life, as it stands today, is the result of choices you've made and actions you've taken or not taken. This realization, while simple in its essence, can serve as a powerful wake-up call.

Consider the story of Thomas Edison, the prolific inventor credited with developing the modern electric light bulb among other inventions. What many people don't know is that his journey to success was not smooth sailing. Before his groundbreaking invention, Edison faced a series of failures. In fact, it's estimated that he failed more than ten thousand times before he finally achieved his goal.

What set Edison apart was his perspective on failure. Rather than viewing these instances as setbacks, he saw each failure as an opportunity to learn, a stepping stone on his path to success. He is famously quoted as saying: "I have not failed. I've just found ten thousand ways that won't work." It was Edison's self-awareness, his recognition of the role action and perseverance played in his life, that propelled him to eventual success.

Exercise: Self-Awareness Reflection

To gain a deeper understanding of the role of action in your own life, try the following exercise:

- Grab a notebook and a pen.

- Write down a goal that you've been striving for but have yet to achieve.

- Reflect on the actions you've taken toward this goal. Write down these actions.

- Reflect on potential actions you could have taken but didn't. Write these down as well.

- Compare the two lists. Are there more actions you could be taking?

This exercise is designed to help you realize the impact of action, or lack thereof, on your personal journey. By doing this, you'll be able to identify areas where more action is required, and you'll gain a better understanding of the power action holds.

Tips for Building Self-Awareness

- **Reflection:** Spend a few minutes each day reflecting on your actions and how they've shaped your day. Reflection leads to self-awareness.

- **Meditation:** Regular meditation can enhance your self-aware-ness by helping you understand your thought patterns and be-havioral tendencies.

- **Journaling:** Keeping a daily journal of your actions and their outcomes can be an excellent tool for increasing self-awareness over time. This practice can offer you insights into your habits, strengths, weaknesses, and areas needing improvement.

Remember, self-awareness is the first step on the path to harnessing the power of action. By understanding and acknowledging the impact of your actions on your current situation, you empower yourself to take charge of your future and shape it according to your desires. You transition from a state of passive existence to one of active creation.

2. Education: Understand the Impact of Action

Once you've recognized the role of action in shaping your life, the next step is to educate yourself about the profound impact of action. Knowledge, as they say, is power. The more you understand about the power of action, the deeper your appreciation for its role in achieving your desired outcomes will be.

The journey of Theodor Seuss Geisel, better known as Dr. Seuss, is an inspiring tale that underscores the power of persistent action. His first book, *And to Think That I Saw It on Mulberry Street*, was rejected by twenty-seven publishers. Discouraged, he considered burning the manuscript, but his determination urged him to continue trying.

He finally found a publisher who was willing to take a chance on his quirky rhymes and whimsical illustrations, leading to the birth of "Dr. Seuss." Today, he is one of the most beloved children's authors in history, with his books being translated into multiple languages and selling millions of copies around the world. His story underlines the impact of action, even in the face of rejection and disappointment.

Exercise: The Action Impact Map

Understanding the impact of action can be achieved through this straightforward exercise:

1. Identify a goal that you have recently achieved and list the specific actions that led to its realization.

2. For each action, identify the outcome it produced, leading you closer to your goal.

3. Reflect on how these outcomes would have been different had you not taken those actions.

By mapping your actions to their outcomes, you'll gain a clearer understanding of the cause-and-effect relationship between action and success. This exercise illustrates the crucial role action plays in bringing about desired changes in your life.

Tips for Enhancing Your Understanding of Action

- **Read Books:** Numerous self-help and motivational books highlight the importance of action. Reading books like *The Power of Now* by Eckhart Tolle or *The 7 Habits of Highly Effective People* by Stephen R. Covey can provide valuable insights into the power of action.

- **Attend Seminars/Webinars:** Participating in seminars or webinars can expose you to different perspectives and success stories, reinforcing the importance of taking action.

- **Learn from Successful People:** There's a wealth of knowledge to be gleaned from individuals who've achieved great things through consistent action. Follow their journeys, absorb their wisdom, and apply it to your life.

Education is the gateway to transformation. As you learn and understand more about the power and impact of action, you equip yourself with the tools needed to construct your path toward success and abundance. Remember, knowledge combined with action is a formidable force that can enable you to turn your dreams into reality.

3. Reflection: Identify Areas for Action

Acknowledging the importance and impact of action, the next crucial step is reflection. Take a moment to delve inward and discern the areas of your life that require action. Self-reflection is a powerful tool for personal growth and advancement. Through mindful exploration, you can gain clarity on the aspects that demand your attention, paving the way for intentional and meaningful action toward your goals. Embrace the power of reflection to identify the specific areas where your actions can make a tangible difference, propelling you forward on your journey toward abundance and success.

Example: Ray Kroc, the visionary behind McDonald's global success, started as a milkshake machine salesman at the age of fifty-two. Observing the highest demand for his product at a single burger stand in California, he decided to pay it a visit. While reflecting on the stand's remarkable success, Kroc identified an opportunity for action—to transform this solitary triumph into a franchise. His reflection led to one of the most groundbreaking business decisions of the twentieth century, showcasing how introspection and identifying areas for action can pave the way for extraordinary achievements.

Exercise: The "Personal Action Mind Map"

A Personal Action Mind Map is a visual tool to represent your thoughts and ideas, helping you organize and understand the different areas of your life that need action. Here's how you can create one:

- **Initiate:** Take a blank sheet of paper and draw a small circle in the center. Label it "My Life."

- **Identify Key Areas:** Think about the different aspects of your life that are important to you — "Health," "Career," "Relationships," "Hobbies," "Education," etc. For each of these aspects, draw a line branching out from the central circle and name that aspect at the end of it.

- **Brainstorm Actions:** Now, under each aspect, brainstorm actions you could take to improve or maintain that aspect. Let your thoughts flow freely, jotting down everything that comes to mind.

- **Visualize and Reflect:** When complete, your mind map will depict a network, akin to a spiderweb of actions radiating out from the central "My Life" circle. Take a moment to reflect on your creation and see what areas need more action from your side.

Example of a "Personal Action Mind Map"

Your Personal Action Mind Map might look something like this:

- Under "Career," you might list actions like "Apply for a promotion," "Update résumé," "Enroll in an online course."

- For "Health," you could write "Join a gym," "Start a meal plan," "Get eight hours of sleep nightly."

- Under "Relationships," actions could include "Schedule weekly date night with spouse," "Call parents every Sunday," "Organize a virtual meet-up with friends."

- For "Personal Development," you could note "Read one book per month," "Learn a new language," "Start a meditation practice."

- Under "Finance," actions might be "Create a budget," "Increase savings by 10 percent," "Invest in stocks."

Your mind map will visually represent a network of actions expanding from the central "My Life" circle. This visual depiction serves as a powerful tool for understanding which actions are necessary to enhance different areas of your life.

Remember, the goal is to help you identify areas that need action. This mind map is a living document of your personal growth journey, so feel free to revisit and update it anytime.

Inspiring Story: J. K. Rowling's Turning Point

Before she became the renowned author of the *Harry Potter* series, J. K. Rowling faced multiple challenges. As a single parent who was unemployed and battling clinical depression, she reached a turning point. Reflecting on her life, Rowling realized that writing was an area she had neglected.

In her own words, she said, "I was set free because my greatest fear had been realized, and I still had a daughter whom I adored, and I had an old typewriter and a big idea. And so rock bottom became a solid foundation on which I rebuilt my life."

Recognizing her passion for writing, J. K. Rowling took decisive action. She focused on bringing to life the book that had been brewing in her mind for years. The rest, as they say, is history.

By reflecting on her circumstances and identifying the area where action was needed, J. K. Rowling transformed her life and created a literary phenomenon. Her story serves as a powerful reminder of the impact reflection and intentional action can have on one's journey of personal growth and success.

Helpful Tips

- **Frequently Update Your Mind Map:** Your life is dynamic and constantly changing. Regularly revisiting and updating your Personal Action Mind Map can help you stay in tune with your needs and aspirations.

- **Be Honest with Yourself:** The effectiveness of your Personal Action Mind Map depends on your honesty. Be truthful about the areas of your life that need action.

- **Consider All Areas:** While it's natural to focus on major areas like career or health, don't neglect smaller areas like hobbies or spiritual life. They can significantly contribute to your overall satisfaction and balance.

- **Use Reflection as a Springboard for Action:** Once you've identified an area needing action, start planning. What small steps can you take to improve this area of your life? Remember, every big journey begins with small steps.

4. Execution: Embrace and Apply the Power of Action

The final stage in understanding the power of action is the most crucial one — execution. It is where understanding, planning, and commitment are transformed into tangible steps and measurable outcomes. Embracing and applying the power of action can lead to extraordinary growth and remarkable success.

Kevin Systrom and Mike Krieger, the founders of Instagram, offer a compelling example of the power of execution through small, iterative actions. In 2010, they launched a location-sharing app called Burbn, which didn't gain much traction. Rather than giving up, they carefully observed user behavior and noticed that people were most engaged with the photo-sharing aspect of Burbn.

Taking action on this insight, they pivoted, focusing their efforts on creating a streamlined photo-sharing app — Instagram. The result was a cultural phenomenon. Instagram's success story underlines the impact of swift, responsive action and the power of executing small, focused changes.

Exercise: The "1% Improvement" Challenge

This exercise is based on the Japanese concept of *kaizen*, which translates to "continuous improvement." The premise is simple: rather than aiming for massive, immediate changes, focus on making small, incremental improvements — just 1 percent each day. Here's how to implement the "1% Improvement" Challenge:

1. Choose an Area for Improvement: Select one aspect of your life where you'd like to see improvement — learning a new language, fitness, productivity at work, etc.

2. Define a Baseline: What does your current effort or performance in this area look like?

3. Plan Your 1%: Identify a way you can improve your current state by just 1% each day. It could be studying an additional minute each day, adding one more push-up to your routine, or spending one more minute focused on your work.

4. Track Your Progress: Make a note of your daily improvements. Over time, you'll be able to see the compound effect of your 1 percent improvements.

5. Celebrate Your Growth: Don't forget to acknowledge and celebrate your progress. This serves as motivation and affirmation of your positive actions.

Inspiring Story: Sarah Breedlove, also known as Madam C. J. Walker

Sarah Breedlove, also known as Madam C. J. Walker, was an extraordinary example of executing goals and aspirations. Born to formerly enslaved parents and facing numerous obstacles, Walker harnessed the power of continuous improvement to change her destiny. She recognized the potential in the hair care industry and developed a groundbreaking product line specifically for Black women.

With a clear vision and unwavering determination, Madam C. J. Walker embarked on her entrepreneurial journey. She implemented the 1% Improvement Challenge, making small, incremental improvements each day to refine her products, expand her customer base, and enhance her business operations. Through her focused execution, she transformed her small-scale enterprise into a thriving business empire.

Madam C. J. Walker's exceptional execution skills propelled her to become one of the first self-made female millionaires in America. Her story exemplifies the transformative power of action and the incredible impact that continuous improvement can have on achieving remarkable success. Let her legacy inspire you to embrace the 1% Improvement Challenge, make daily strides toward your goals, and execute with unwavering determination.

Helpful Tips

- **Maintain Consistency:** The power of 1 percent improvements lies in their cumulative effect over time. Stay consistent in your efforts.

- **Avoid Perfectionism:** The goal is improvement, not perfection. Some days, you may not manage your 1 percent improvement — and that's okay. The key is to keep trying.

- **Stay Patient:** Major changes won't happen overnight. The "1% Improvement" Challenge is a marathon, not a sprint. Trust the process.

By focusing on small, manageable improvements, you can create significant change over time. This approach makes the process of taking action less daunting and more achievable, allowing you yours, and the time is now. Take action and embark on this transformative journey toward success, abundance, and the fulfillment of your deepest aspirations.

The Power of Action in Transforming Dreams into Reality

Imagine a world where dreams exist only as fleeting thoughts, forever trapped within the confines of your mind. It is action that holds the key to liberation, transforming those dreams from intangible fantasies into concrete manifestations. Action becomes the driving force that propels you forward, infusing your aspirations with purpose and direction.

Consider the awe-inspiring journey of Anne Sullivan and Helen Keller, a tale that vividly showcases the Power of Action in Transforming Dreams into Reality. Helen Keller, at a tender age, found herself confined within a silent and dark world, devoid of communication and understanding. Yet, it was through the unwavering dedication and tireless action of Anne Sullivan, her remarkable teacher, that Helen's world began to expand.

With boundless patience, unwavering persistence, and countless hours of instruction, Anne Sullivan taught Helen to communicate through sign language, opening the doors to her potential and paving the way for her extraordinary achievements. Helen Keller's remarkable story stands as a testament to the life-altering impact of action, a resounding testament that proves even the most unimaginable feats can be accomplished through unyielding determination and action.

Despite profound disabilities, Helen Keller made a remarkable difference in the world through her advocacy and accomplishments. She became a renowned author, lecturer, and political activist, dedicating her life to improving the lives of individuals with disabilities and promoting social change. Keller was the first deaf-blind person to earn a bachelor of arts degree, and she tirelessly campaigned for the rights and education of people with disabilities. Through her writings and speeches, she inspired countless individuals, challenging societal perceptions and advocating for equal opportunities. Helen Keller's indomitable spirit and determination continue to inspire generations, leaving an enduring legacy of resilience and the power of overcoming obstacles.

May this remarkable tale of Helen Keller inspire you to unleash the transformative power of action in your own life, to break free from the confines of doubt and uncertainty, and to embark on a journey that transforms your dreams into reality. Remember, it is through action that you ignite the fire within, propelling you toward a future where the unimaginable becomes attainable.

The Feedback Loop of Learning and Adaptation

Action not only brings us closer to our goals but also sets in motion a powerful feedback loop of learning and adaptation. Each action we take provides valuable insights and feedback, allowing us to adjust our course, refine our strategies, and improve our outcomes. It is through action that we learn, grow, and evolve on our journey toward success.

Consider the story of Malala Yousafzai, a young Pakistani activist who fought for girls' education in the face of extreme adversity. Growing up in the Swat Valley of Pakistan, Malala witnessed the Taliban's oppressive rule and their efforts to restrict girls' access to education.

Rather than remaining silent, Malala took courageous action by speaking out against the injustice. She began advocating for girls' education through a blog and media interviews, despite facing threats and dangers. Her activism gained international attention, and she became a symbol of bravery and resilience.

Tragically, in 2012, Malala was targeted by the Taliban and shot in the head. However, her spirit and determination were not shattered. Instead, her near-death experience fueled her resolve to continue her fight for education and empowerment.

Malala's story showcases the transformative power of action in the pursuit of a noble cause. Her actions sparked a global movement, and she became the youngest-ever Nobel Prize laureate, receiving the Nobel Peace Prize at the age of seventeen.

The story of Malala Yousafzai highlights that action, even in the face of immense challenges, can bring about profound change. It teaches us that no matter our age or circumstances, we have the power to take action and make a difference in the world.

By sharing stories like Malala's, we are reminded of the importance of action in our own lives. Each of us has the potential to create positive change, no matter how small our actions may seem. It is through our actions that we shape our destiny and contribute to the betterment of society.

Let Malala's story inspire you to take action, stand up for what you believe in, and work toward a more just and equitable world. Together, our collective actions can bring about meaningful and lasting impact.

Overcoming Inertia and Building Momentum

Taking that first step into action can be challenging. Often, we find ourselves caught in the grip of inertia, hesitating to venture beyond our comfort zones. But it is in those moments of decision and action that true transformation begins.

One powerful example of overcoming inertia and building momentum is the story of Rosa Parks. In a time of deep-seated racial segregation, Rosa's simple act of refusing to give up her bus seat to a white passenger sparked a flame of resistance that spread like wildfire. Her courageous action became the catalyst for the Montgomery bus boycott, a pivotal moment in the civil rights movement.

Parks's defiance against injustice empowered countless others to join the cause, to stand up against discrimination, and to fight for equality. Each person who took part in the boycott contributed to a growing wave of momentum, a force that could no longer be ignored.

This story of Rosa Parks reminds us that even the smallest acts of courage and resistance can lead to profound change. Each action we take, no matter how seemingly insignificant, has the potential to create a ripple effect, inspiring others and building a movement. With each step forward, we gain momentum, our passion and determination growing stronger.

So, when faced with the daunting task of taking action, remember the power of Rosa Parks's bold stand. Embrace the challenge, overcome inertia, and trust that your actions, no matter how small, can be the spark that ignites a movement and leads to transformative change.

Harnessing the Power of Action: Your Path to Abundance and Success

To harness the transformative power of action, it must be embraced as a daily practice. Here are some key steps to guide you on your journey:

Cultivate a Growth Mindset: Adopting a growth mindset is crucial for taking meaningful action. Embrace the belief that your abilities and intelligence can be developed through effort and perseverance. Embrace challenges as opportunities for growth, view obstacles as stepping stones, and see failures as valuable feedback. With a growth mindset, you'll approach action with a sense of resilience and a willingness to learn from every experience.

Embody Courage and Boldness: Taking action requires courage and a willingness to step outside of your comfort zone. Embrace the discomfort that comes with uncertainty, and take bold steps toward your goals. Remember, greatness lies beyond the boundaries of familiarity. Be willing to take risks, face your fears, and challenge the status quo. It is through courageous action that you'll discover new possibilities and unleash your true potential.

Practice Discipline and Consistency: Discipline and consistency are the fuel that keeps your actions moving forward. Develop daily habits and routines that support your goals. Create a schedule that allows you to allocate time and energy for the actions that matter most. Embrace the power of consistency, knowing that small, consistent actions compound over time and lead to remarkable results.

Embrace Resilience and Perseverance: Action is often met with obstacles and setbacks. Embrace the mindset of resilience and perseverance. When faced with challenges, see them as opportunities to test your resolve and adapt your approach. Cultivate resilience by bouncing back from failures, learning from them, and using setbacks as stepping stones to propel you forward. Remember, success rarely comes without perseverance and the determination to keep going, no matter the circumstances.

Tap into Your Inner Motivation: Find your personal motivation that drives you to take action. Understand your "why" — the deep-rooted purpose and passion behind your goals. Connect with your values and aspirations and let them fuel your actions. When you align your actions with your core values and inner motivation, you tap into an endless source of energy and inspiration.

Reflect and Learn from Your Actions: Regularly reflect on your actions and evaluate their effectiveness. Take time to analyze what worked well and what could be improved. Learn from both successes and failures, and apply those lessons to refine your future actions. By continuously learning and adapting, you'll optimize your approach and increase your chances of success.

By shifting the focus to the mindset and attitude that drives effective action, you will be empowered with a fresh perspective and inspired to take meaningful steps toward your goals. This approach encourages a holistic understanding of action, beyond just the practical steps, and enables you to cultivate the mindset necessary for consistent and purposeful action.

Inspiring Story: Chadwick Boseman's Legacy

Chadwick Boseman, the late actor known for his iconic portrayal of Black Panther, left a profound impact through his actions on and off the screen. Despite battling cancer in secret, Boseman continued to take on challenging roles and deliver powerful performances. His dedication, perseverance, and commitment to his craft inspired millions around the world.

Boseman once said, "The only difference between a hero and the villain is that the villain chooses to use that power in a way that is selfish and hurts other people." He understood the power of his actions and used his platform to champion representation, equality, and justice. Boseman's legacy serves as a reminder that our actions have the potential to leave a lasting impact, shaping not only our own lives but also the lives of others.

By taking consistent action, embracing failure as a learning opportunity, seeking inspiration, and celebrating your wins, you can harness the power of action and set yourself on the path to abundance and success. Remember, your dreams are within reach, but it is through your actions that they become a reality. Embrace the transformative power of action, and let it propel you toward a future filled with endless possibilities.

The Mindset for Action: Unleashing the Power Within

In the grand symphony of life, the melody of our thoughts resonates through every action we take. Within the depths of our minds, dreams find fertile ground to sprout, aspirations come alive, and the potential for abundance and success takes root. To embark on a transformative journey of action, we must nurture a mindset that propels us forward, kindles the flames of our passions, and fuels unwavering determination. It is this very mindset that unlocks the door to our true potential and sets us on the path to fulfillment.

Consider the inspiring story of Maya Angelou, a renowned poet, author, and civil rights activist. Angelou's life journey is a testament to the transformative power of a determined mindset and consistent action.

Growing up in a challenging environment marked by racial discrimination and trauma, Angelou faced numerous obstacles on her path to success. However, she refused to be defined by her circumstances and instead embraced a mindset of resilience and unwavering determination.

Through her love for literature and poetry, Angelou discovered her passion and used it as a catalyst for change. She used her words to shed light on the injustices and inequalities she witnessed, and her powerful voice became a symbol of hope and inspiration for generations to come.

Angelou's journey was not without its setbacks and failures, but she never allowed them to deter her. She understood that action was the key to progress and growth. With each setback, she learned valuable lessons, adapted her approach, and persisted in pursuing her dreams.

Through her consistent action and unwavering belief in herself, Angelou achieved remarkable success. She became the first African American woman to write a best-selling nonfiction book, *I Know Why the Caged Bird Sings*, and went on to publish numerous acclaimed works.

Angelou's story teaches us the power of a determined mindset and consistent action in the pursuit of our goals. It reminds us that no matter the challenges we face, we have the ability to rise above them and create a meaningful impact through our actions.

By drawing inspiration from Angelou's journey, we can cultivate a mindset of resilience, embrace our unique talents and passions, and take consistent action toward our aspirations. It is through our unwavering belief in ourselves and our commitment to action that we can overcome obstacles and create a life of abundance and success.

Beyond the realm of literature, let's turn our attention to the world of sports and the story of Serena Williams, labeled as "The Greatest" in *Time* magazine's September 2022 issue. Widely regarded as the greatest tennis player of all time, Williams has achieved remarkable success through her unwavering determination and mental fortitude.

In the face of intense competition, injuries, and personal setbacks, Williams exemplifies the mindset of a champion. She maintains an unshakable belief in her abilities, relentlessly pushes herself to new heights, and embraces the challenges that come with being at the top of her game. Williams's mindset, coupled with her actions and work ethic, has propelled her to numerous Grand Slam victories and solidified her status as a true icon in the world of sports.

These narratives, among countless others, serve as reminders that the mindset we adopt shapes our actions and, in turn, our destiny. It is a mindset that recognizes the power of belief, resilience, and determination — the core ingredients for unleashing our full potential.

To cultivate a mindset for action, we must first embrace the power of self-belief. It is the unwavering confidence in our abilities, our dreams, and our capacity to overcome obstacles that propels us forward. As Henry Ford once said, "Whether you think you can or you think you can't, you're right." Our beliefs have the power to shape our reality, and by adopting a mindset of possibility and self-assurance, we set the stage for taking bold and decisive action.

Alongside self-belief, the mindset for action embraces a spirit of adaptability and resilience. Life is filled with unexpected twists and turns, and it is our ability to adapt to new circumstances, learn from setbacks, and persist in the face of challenges that determines our ultimate success. Each setback becomes an opportunity for growth and learning, and with a mindset focused on continuous improvement, we become more adept at navigating the ever-changing landscape of our goals and aspirations.

Moreover, a mindset for action acknowledges the power of purpose and passion. When our actions are aligned with our deepest values, when they resonate with our authentic selves, they become infused with an unparalleled sense of meaning and fulfillment. It is through this alignment that our actions become purpose-driven, igniting a fire within us that fuels our dedication and commitment.

As we embark on our own personal journeys of action, it is crucial to surround ourselves with positive influences and seek inspiration from those who have achieved greatness through their actions. By engaging with stories of individuals who have overcome adversity, defied odds, and made a lasting impact, we expand our own realm of possibility and reinforce our belief in the transformative power of action.

In addition to external sources of inspiration, cultivating a supportive and empowering internal dialogue is paramount. The way we speak to ourselves shapes our mindset and influences our actions. Replace self-doubt and self-criticism with self-compassion and self-encouragement.

Treat yourself with kindness and remind yourself of your inherent worth and potential. By nurturing a positive and empowering inner dialogue, you create a fertile ground for action to flourish.

Another essential aspect of the mindset for action is embracing a growth-oriented perspective. Recognize that every experience, whether it brings success or failure, holds valuable lessons and opportunities for growth. Embrace challenges as stepping stones on your journey rather than insurmountable barriers. Approach setbacks as temporary detours that can lead to new insights and alternative paths. With a growth mindset, you cultivate resilience, adaptability, and a hunger for continuous improvement.

A mindset for action also involves developing a sense of ownership and responsibility for your own life. Understand that you have the power to shape your destiny and that your actions have a direct impact on your outcomes. Rather than waiting for circumstances to align perfectly or for external validation, take the initiative and responsibility for your choices and actions. Embrace the autonomy to create your own path and be proactive in pursuing your goals.

To reinforce the mindset for action, practice visualization and affirmations. Visualize yourself taking decisive steps toward your goals, achieving success, and experiencing the abundant life you desire. Affirmations are powerful statements that reinforce positive beliefs and attitudes. Repeat affirmations that align with your aspirations, such as "I am capable of achieving my dreams," "I embrace challenges as opportunities for growth," or "I am deserving of abundance and success." By consistently engaging in visualization and affirmations, you rewire your subconscious mind and strengthen your belief in your ability to take action and create the life you envision.

Lastly, surround yourself with a supportive community that shares your values and aspirations. Seek out like-minded individuals who inspire and uplift you. Engage in discussions, collaborate on projects, and share experiences with those who are on a similar path of personal growth and action. The collective energy and support of a community can provide encouragement, accountability, and fresh perspectives that fuel your motivation and help you overcome obstacles.

As you embrace the mindset for action, recognize that it is not a static state but an ongoing process of growth and self-discovery. It requires consistent effort, self-reflection, and a willingness to challenge limiting beliefs and step outside your comfort zones. By adopting a mindset that empowers you to take action, you unleash the full potential within and set the stage for a life of abundance, fulfillment, and success.

Upcoming sections will delve deeper into the practical strategies and techniques that complement this empowering mindset, providing the tools and guidance to take decisive action toward your goals. Remember, your mindset is the catalyst that transforms your dreams into reality. Embrace the power of your thoughts, align them with purposeful action, and witness the extraordinary impact they can have on your journey toward abundance and success.

Recognizing and Overcoming Barriers: Fear, Perfectionism, and Procrastination

Taking action can be daunting, often hindered by common barriers such as fear, perfectionism, and procrastination. Fear of failure or judgment can paralyze us, keeping us stuck in our comfort zones. Perfectionism can lead to excessive self-criticism and unrealistic expectations, preventing us from taking the necessary steps forward. Procrastination, the tendency to delay action, can be a result of anxiety or a fear of making mistakes. To overcome these barriers, it's important to develop awareness and take these proactive steps:

- **Acknowledge your fears:** Recognize that fear is a natural response to venturing into the unknown. Understand that growth and progress often require stepping outside your comfort zone. By acknowledging your fears and reframing them as opportunities for growth, you can gradually diminish their power over you.

- **Embrace imperfection:** Understand that perfection is an unattainable ideal. Embrace the concept of "progress over perfection" and allow yourself to make mistakes along the way. View failures as learning experiences that contribute to your growth and development.

- **Break tasks into manageable steps:** Procrastination often arises from feeling overwhelmed by the enormity of a task. Break down your goals into smaller, manageable steps. Focus on one step at a time, celebrating each milestone achieved along the way. This approach helps alleviate the pressure and builds momentum toward action.

Unleashing the Power of Mindset for Action

The right mindset lays the foundation for effective action. It's the internal compass that guides our thoughts, beliefs, and behaviors as we embark on our journey toward abundance and success. Cultivating a mindset that supports action requires us to address common barriers such as fear, perfectionism, and procrastination. By incorporating mindfulness techniques, reframing strategies, and drawing inspiration from transformative stories, we can shift our mindset and embrace the path of action.

1. Confront Fear: Fear often paralyzes us and prevents us from taking action. However, we can reframe fear as an opportunity for growth and transformation. Recognize that fear is a natural response to stepping outside our comfort zones. By acknowledging our fears and understanding that they are part of the process, we can cultivate the courage to move forward. Embrace fear as a sign of progress, and let it fuel your determination rather than hinder your actions.

2. Overcome Perfectionism: Perfectionism can be a significant barrier to action. The relentless pursuit of flawlessness often leads to procrastination and a fear of failure. Instead, shift your perspective and embrace the concept of "progress over perfec-

tion." Recognize that taking imperfect action is far more valuable than endlessly seeking perfection. Embrace the idea that mistakes and setbacks are opportunities for growth and learning. Emphasize progress, learning, and iterative improvement rather than seeking flawless outcomes.

3. Defeat Procrastination: Procrastination can derail even the best-laid plans. To overcome it, practice mindfulness and develop a sense of urgency for action. Break tasks into smaller, manageable steps, and set realistic deadlines. Visualize the positive outcomes of taking action and the potential consequences of procrastination. Build momentum by starting with small, achievable tasks and gradually increasing the level of challenge. By taking consistent action, you'll build a habit of productivity and overcome the grip of procrastination.

4. Embrace Inspired Action: Beyond addressing barriers, we can tap into the power of inspired action. Seek inspiration from individuals who have transformed their lives through action. Explore stories of ordinary people who dared to defy limitations and achieved extraordinary results. Reflect on their journeys, internalize their mindset, and draw motivation from their triumphs. Allow their narratives to ignite the spark within you, propelling you to take action and unleash your true potential.

5. Adopt a Solution-Oriented Mindset: Cultivate a mindset focused on solutions rather than dwelling on problems. Shift your perspective from seeing obstacles as roadblocks to viewing them as opportunities for creative problem-solving. Embrace a growth mindset that embraces challenges and approaches them with curiosity and determination. Instead of being overwhelmed by difficulties, see them as invitations to develop new skills, acquire knowledge, and expand your capabilities.

6. Practice Mindfulness and Self-Reflection: Incorporate mindfulness techniques to enhance self-awareness and develop a deeper understanding of your thoughts, emotions, and behaviors. En-

gage in regular self-reflection to identify any self-limiting beliefs or patterns that hinder your progress. Cultivate self-compassion and treat yourself with kindness and understanding. By nurturing mindfulness and self-reflection, you'll cultivate a heightened awareness of your actions and align them with your aspirations.

By addressing fear, overcoming perfectionism and procrastination, embracing inspired action, adopting a solution-oriented mindset, and practicing mindfulness and self-reflection, you can cultivate a powerful mindset for action. Embrace the transformative potential that lies within you, and let your mindset propel you forward on the path to abundance and success. Remember, action is not just a choice—it is a catalyst for change, a vehicle that propels you toward the life you envision. It is through intentional and purposeful action that you bridge the gap between where you are and where you want to be. By cultivating a mindset that embraces action, you empower yourself to break free from the shackles of stagnation and make meaningful progress toward your goals.

As you embark on your journey of personal growth and achievement, embody the mindset of a lifelong learner, always seeking opportunities for growth and improvement. Embrace the challenges that come your way, viewing them as stepping stones on the path to success. And remember that action, no matter how small, has the power to create ripples of positive change that extend far beyond your own life.

So, dare to dream big, but also dare to take bold action! Step out of your comfort zone, confront your fears, and silence the voice of self-doubt. Embrace imperfection, knowing that progress is more important than perfection. Break the cycle of procrastination by infusing your actions with a sense of purpose and urgency.

Remember, it is not enough to simply desire change. It is through action that desires are manifested and brought into reality. So seize the power of the present moment, embrace the mindset for action, and embark on this remarkable adventure toward the fulfillment of your true potential.

Inspiring Narratives: Shifting Mindsets and Embracing Action

Drawing inspiration from real-life stories can provide powerful examples of individuals who shifted their mindsets and embraced action to achieve remarkable success. Here are additional narratives to inspire you:

a. The story of Sara Blakely, the founder of Spanx, serves as a testament to the transformative power of a growth mindset. Blakely encountered countless obstacles and rejections while developing her innovative shapewear concept. However, she persisted with a mindset that saw failure as an opportunity for growth. Eventually, her unwavering belief in her product paid off, leading to the creation of a billion-dollar company that revolutionized the undergarment industry.

b. Consider the journey of Mahatma Gandhi, a leader who championed nonviolent resistance and played a pivotal role in India's struggle for independence. Gandhi's mindset of unwavering determination and resilience drove him to take action, even in the face of immense adversity. His approach to nonviolent activism, coupled with a profound belief in justice and equality, transformed the course of history and inspired generations.

By immersing ourselves in narratives like these, we gain valuable insights into the transformative power of mindset and action. They remind us that our thoughts and beliefs shape our actions, and by adopting a growth mindset and embracing action, we, too, can overcome challenges and create the life we envision.

Cultivating the right mindset for action is crucial on the path to abundance. By recognizing and overcoming barriers, cultivating a growth mindset, incorporating mindfulness techniques, and drawing inspiration from inspiring narratives, you equip yourself with the mental and emotional readiness necessary to take effective action. Remember, your mindset is a powerful force that can propel you toward your goals. Embrace the possibilities, step out of your comfort zone, and harness the mindset that empowers you to take bold and purposeful action toward a future filled with endless potential.

Actionable Steps for Achieving Abundance and Success

Amid the vast expanse of possibilities that life presents, dreams of abundance and success call out to us like whispers of a captivating tale waiting to unfold. Yet these dreams remain insubstantial unless we seize the reins of destiny and embark on a deliberate and purposeful journey. It is through intentional and focused action that we breathe life into our aspirations, molding them into tangible realities that surpass even our most vivid imaginings.

In this transformative section, we continue onward, navigating through the profound exploration of actionable steps that will empower you to embark on your own personal odyssey toward abundance and success. Here, we delve into the depths of practical guidance, interwoven with inspiring narratives of individuals who have harnessed the power of action to forge their own destinies. Together, we will unearth the tools and wisdom needed to sculpt a solid foundation upon which your path to abundance can be built.

With each step you take, you will unravel the threads of doubt and uncertainty, weaving a tapestry of purpose and fulfillment that reflects your unique vision. Guided by these actionable steps, you will navigate the labyrinth of choices, overcoming obstacles and surmounting challenges that threaten to derail your progress. Through unwavering commitment and a steadfast belief in your own potential, you will unlock the door to a realm where dreams intertwine seamlessly with reality.

Are you ready to embark on an extraordinary journey? Are you prepared to embrace the power within you and chart a course toward a life of abundance and success? If so, then let us embark on this transformative adventure together. Within these pages, you will find the keys that unlock the vast potential residing within your very being.

It is time to seize this remarkable opportunity and script a narrative that transcends the ordinary, defies expectations, and soars on the wings of your courageous action. Together, we will venture into the heart of action, where dreams take shape, where aspirations are woven into the very fabric of existence, and where the extraordinary becomes an inherent part of your everyday reality.

In this profound exploration, we embark on the path where mere dreams are transformed into tangible achievements. We navigate the intricate tapestry of life, skillfully weaving purpose and passion into every step we take. Through deliberate and focused action, we shatter the limitations that confine us, unlocking the true masterpiece of our lives. Together, we will uncover the tools, insights, and wisdom needed to carve out our own destinies and create a life that surpasses our wildest dreams.

Are you ready to boldly step forward on the path to abundance? Then let us join forces and embark on this transformative adventure. Within these pages lies the guiding light that will illuminate your path. With every stride, you will breathe life into your aspirations, infusing them with unwavering determination and unwavering belief. You will unleash the power of action and create a symphony of success that resonates through every fiber of your being.

Now is the time to rise above mediocrity, transcend the limitations that hold you back, and forge a destiny that is uniquely yours. Step forward with courage and conviction, for the world eagerly awaits the manifestation of your extraordinary potential. As you follow this path, you will navigate the labyrinth of possibilities, guided by the unwavering belief that within you lies the capacity to achieve greatness.

So take a deep breath, summon your inner strength, and let us embark on this transformative journey toward abundance and success. Together, we will unleash the power of action and author a story that echoes through eternity.

Step 1: Define Your Vision

Having a clear vision of what you desire is an essential first step to achieving success and abundance. Take time to reflect on your dreams, aspirations, and goals. What does abundance mean to you? How do you envision success? Write down your vision in vivid detail, allowing your imagination to paint a picture of your ideal future. This exercise will give you a concrete target to aim for and serve as a guiding light throughout your journey.

Inspiring Story: The Visionary Leader

Imagine the extraordinary journey of Rev. Johnnie Coleman, a visionary leader and spiritual teacher who left an indelible mark on the world through her actions and teachings. Rev. Coleman founded the Universal Foundation for Better Living and became a pioneer in the New Thought movement, empowering countless individuals to transform their lives through spiritual principles and conscious action.

Born and raised in the racially segregated South, Rev. Coleman faced numerous challenges and injustices. However, she refused to let her circumstances define her. Instead, she embraced a mindset of possibility, resilience, and love and set out to create positive change.

Through her teachings and actions, Rev. Coleman inspired others to recognize their inherent worth, tap into their inner power, and live their lives with intention and purpose. She believed that every person has the capacity to shape their reality through their thoughts, beliefs, and actions.

Rev. Coleman's journey was characterized by a deep commitment to personal growth and self-discovery. She continuously sought wisdom and expanded her understanding of spiritual principles, incorporating them into her own life and sharing them with others.

Through her unwavering belief in the power of spiritual transformation, Rev. Coleman created a global movement that touched the lives of countless individuals. Her teachings emphasized the importance of aligning thoughts, words, and actions with one's highest values and aspirations.

Rev. Coleman's actions demonstrated the transformative power of intentional living. She encouraged her followers to take responsibility for their own lives and make choices that aligned with their authentic selves. Through her guidance, people were empowered to overcome limitations, embrace their divine potential, and create lives filled with abundance, joy, and love.

Rev. Coleman's legacy serves as a reminder that action, fueled by a deep sense of purpose and aligned with spiritual principles, can bring about profound and lasting change. Her story inspires us to harness the power within ourselves, embark on our own spiritual journeys, and take action to create the lives we envision.

As we reflect on Rev. Johnnie Coleman's life, let us be inspired to embrace conscious action in our own lives. Let her story be a catalyst for personal transformation, as we align our thoughts, beliefs, and actions with our highest ideals. By following in her footsteps, we can tap into our inner power, manifest our dreams, and make a positive impact in the world.

Rev. Johnnie Coleman's story is a testament to the transformative power of action and the immense potential within each of us. Let us honor her legacy by stepping into our own power, igniting the fullness of our potential, taking inspired action, and creating a conscious life of purpose, joy, prosperity, and abundance.

Step 2: Unleash the Power of Inspired Action

Once the flame of your clear and inspiring vision has been ignited, it is time to harness the transformative power of inspired action. Rather than merely crafting a path, you are invited to embark on a remarkable journey of purposeful and soul-stirring action. This step transcends the conventional notions of strategic planning and instead focuses on tapping into your inner well of passion, creativity, and intuition to propel you toward your goals.

Practical Exercise: Igniting Your Inspired Action

1. Awaken Your Inner Fire: Take a moment to reconnect with the burning passion that resides within you. Reflect on the deepest desires and aspirations that drive your vision. Immerse yourself in the emotions and sensations associated with the fulfillment of your goals. Let this fiery energy fuel your action.

2. Embrace Your Unique Strengths: Recognize and honor the unique strengths, talents, and gifts you possess. Identify how you can leverage these qualities to make a meaningful impact and move closer to your vision. Embrace the power of authenticity, and let your true self shine through your actions.

3. Seek Inspiration from Unexpected Sources: Look beyond the traditional sources of inspiration. Explore diverse disciplines, industries, and cultures that may offer fresh perspectives and innovative approaches. Seek out stories, experiences, and ideas that challenge your assumptions and spark new insights.

4. Cultivate Mindful Action: Infuse your actions with a sense of mindfulness and presence. Be fully engaged in the present moment, savoring each step of your journey. By cultivating this awareness, you deepen your connection to your vision and ensure that your actions are purposeful and aligned with your values.

5. Embrace Boldness and Take Calculated Risks: Step out of your comfort zone and embrace the exhilarating realm of calculated risks. Identify opportunities that stretch your limits and allow for transformative growth. Embrace the possibility of failure as a valuable learning experience on the path to success.

6. Foster Collaboration and Connection: Recognize that your journey is not a solitary one. Surround yourself with a supportive

network of individuals who share your vision or possess complementary skills and perspectives. Collaborate, exchange ideas, and support each other in achieving mutual success.

7. Harness the Power of Intuition: Tap into your intuition, that subtle and often overlooked inner guidance system. Quiet the noise of external influences and listen to the whispers of your intuition. Trust your instincts, for they can provide profound insights and guide you to make inspired decisions.

8. Celebrate Progress and Practice Gratitude: Along your journey, take moments to celebrate your achievements, no matter how small. Recognize the progress you have made, and express gratitude for the opportunities, resources, and support that have come your way. Cultivating gratitude amplifies the positive energy and keeps you aligned with abundance.

By embracing the power of inspired action, you infuse your journey with passion, creativity, and purpose. Let your heart guide your steps, and let your actions become a symphony of transformative change. Stay attuned to the rhythm of your vision, and let it propel you forward on this extraordinary adventure toward abundance and success.

Through this practical exercise, immerse yourself in the realm of inspired action. Ignite your inner fire, embrace your unique strengths, seek unconventional inspiration, foster mindful engagement, embrace calculated risks, nurture collaboration, listen to your intuition, and celebrate your progress. With each inspired action you take, you harness the power to create a life that surpasses your wildest dreams.

Inspiring Story: The Fiery Trailblazer

Imagine Sofia, a young woman who grew up in a small, impoverished village, filled with limitations and adversity. Despite her circumstances, Sofia possessed a burning passion for education, empowerment, and a better future. Her unwavering determination led her to excel academically and secure a scholarship to study engineering at a prestigious university.

During her time at university, Sofia discovered her true calling: renewable energy. She realized the immense potential of clean energy to create sustainable progress and transform communities. Driven by her vision, Sofia embarked on a mission to bring affordable and clean energy solutions to underserved areas.

Sofia faced numerous challenges along her journey. She encountered skepticism, financial constraints, and technical hurdles. However, her fiery spirit propelled her forward, refusing to let anything extinguish her inner flame.

Drawing inspiration from the sun's boundless energy, Sofia became a trailblazer in solar technology. Through her relentless research and collaboration with experts, she developed a breakthrough solar technology named Radiance Solar. This innovative solution harnessed sunlight in the most efficient and cost-effective way, with the potential to provide electricity to remote communities and drive sustainable development.

Armed with a prototype, Sofia embarked on a journey to demonstrate the impact of her invention. She traveled to remote villages, witnessing firsthand the transformative power of electricity in people's lives. This experience fueled her determination to reach more communities and make an even greater difference.

Sofia's groundbreaking invention caught the attention of investors, philanthropists, and changemakers who recognized its potential. With their support, Sofia established Solara Tech, a social enterprise dedicated to bringing her solar solution to communities worldwide.

Word spread rapidly about Sofia's innovation, attracting partnerships with governments, NGOs, and communities. Sofia's social enterprise flourished, attracting a team of passionate individuals who shared her vision and dedication. Together, they set up solar power grids, trained local technicians, and empowered communities to embrace their energy future.

Sofia's innovation not only provided electricity but also opened doors to education, health care, and economic opportunities previously unimaginable. Her journey serves as a testament to the power of passion, determination, and a belief in the potential of ideas.

Let Sofia's story ignite your own fiery spirit and inspire you to take action, challenge your boundaries, create change, and pursue your visions with tenacity and resilience. Her journey exemplifies the potential within each of us to be trailblazers, catalysts for positive transformation, and architects of a brighter and greener world.

Step 3: Take Consistent Action

Action without consistency often leads to stagnation. To achieve abundance and success, it is vital to take consistent, purposeful action. Identify the key actions that will propel you toward your goals, and commit to executing them on a regular basis. Create a schedule or routine that incorporates these actions into your daily, weekly, and monthly life. Embrace the power of consistency, knowing that each action you take builds momentum and brings you closer to your desired outcomes.

Inspiring Story: Eliud Kipchoge – The Marathon Maestro

Eliud Kipchoge, a Kenyan long-distance runner, is widely regarded as one of the greatest marathon runners of all time. His relentless pursuit of excellence and dedication to taking consistent action have led him to achieve remarkable feats in the world of athletics.

Kipchoge's most notable achievement came on October 12, 2019, when he became the first person in history to complete a marathon in under two hours. This incredible feat, known as the "INEOS 1:59 Challenge," showcased Kipchoge's exceptional endurance and unwavering commitment to pushing the boundaries of human potential.

Behind this historic accomplishment lies years of consistent action and training. Kipchoge's rigorous training regimen involves logging hundreds of miles each week, adhering to a strict diet, and maintaining a disciplined lifestyle. He consistently puts in the work, day after day, month after month, year after year, to enhance his physical and mental capabilities.

Kipchoge's dedication to taking consistent action extends beyond training. He approaches each race with a meticulous strategy and unwavering focus, emphasizing the importance of pacing, form, and mental fortitude. Through disciplined training and race-day execution, Kipchoge has dominated the marathon scene, setting numerous world records and winning numerous prestigious titles.

What sets Kipchoge apart is not only his athletic prowess but also his mindset. He firmly believes in the power of the human spirit and the ability to achieve the seemingly impossible through consistent action and a positive mindset. Kipchoge often emphasizes the importance of self-belief, hard work, and discipline as key ingredients for success.

Kipchoge's story serves as a powerful reminder that taking consistent action, combined with a resilient mindset, can lead to extraordinary achievements. It underscores the significance of setting ambitious goals, maintaining discipline, and persistently working toward them, even in the face of challenges and setbacks.

In the context of *The Wealth Spark*, Kipchoge's story highlights the importance of consistency and perseverance in pursuing our goals. Just as Kipchoge continually strives for excellence in his sport, we, too, must take consistent action, maintain discipline, and stay focused on our objectives.

Let Kipchoge's story inspire you to embody the spirit of taking consistent action in your pursuit of abundance and success. By maintaining a steadfast commitment to your goals and consistently putting in the effort, you can overcome obstacles and achieve remarkable results, transforming your life and future.

Step 4: Ignite Your Growth Potential

Within each of us lies the untapped potential for growth and transformation. Cultivating a growth mindset is the key to unlocking this potential and propelling yourself toward abundance and success. A growth mindset is the belief that your abilities and intelligence can be developed through effort, learning, and perseverance. It is about embracing challenges, seeking opportunities for growth, and persistently expanding your skills and knowledge.

Practical Exercise: Unleashing Your Growth Mindset

1. Embrace the Power of "Yet": Whenever you encounter a challenge or feel like you have not achieved something yet, remind yourself that it is a temporary state. Replace statements like "I can't do it" with "I can't do it *yet*." Embrace the idea that with time, effort, and learning, you can overcome any obstacle and achieve your goals.

2. Embody a Curious Learner's Attitude: Cultivate a sense of curiosity and a hunger for knowledge. Approach every experience with an open mind, seeking to learn and grow. Embrace the joy of discovering innovative ideas, perspectives, and skills. See setbacks as opportunities to learn rather than as failures, and adjust your course.

3. Embrace the Power of "Not Yet": When faced with a setback or a perceived failure, reframe your thinking. Instead of seeing it as a permanent defeat, view it as a "not yet" moment. Recognize that setbacks are part of the growth process and provide valuable insights and lessons. Learn from them, adapt your strategies, and keep moving forward.

4. **Surround Yourself with Growth-Minded Individuals:** Seek out and connect with individuals who have a growth mindset. Surrounding yourself with people who believe in growth and development will inspire and motivate you. Engage in meaningful conversations, share experiences, and support each other's journeys of growth.

5. **Set Stretch Goals:** Challenge yourself by setting stretch goals that push you beyond your comfort zone. Aim for goals that are slightly beyond what you believe is currently attainable. By striving for these goals, you expand your capabilities, develop new skills, and foster a growth mindset that embraces continuous improvement.

6. **Foster Collaborative Learning:** Surround yourself with a diverse community of learners who share your passion for personal growth and success. Engage in group discussions, workshops, or online forums where you can exchange ideas, share insights, and learn from one another. Embrace the power of collective wisdom and leverage the knowledge and experiences of others to expand your own understanding and perspectives.

7. **Harness the Power of Visualization:** Utilize the power of visualization to enhance your growth mindset journey. Take time to vividly imagine yourself achieving your goals, experiencing the emotions and sensations associated with success. Visualize the steps you need to take, the challenges you may encounter, and the actions you will implement to overcome them. By regularly visualizing your desired outcomes, you reinforce positive beliefs and prime your mind for success, strengthening your commitment to growth and inspiring greater action.

Inspiring Story: The Masterpiece Unveiled

In the bustling city of Florence, a young artist named Michelangelo dreamed of creating masterpieces that would stand the test of time.

From a tender age, he possessed an insatiable thirst for knowledge and an unwavering commitment to honing his craft.

Michelangelo's journey was not without challenges. Despite coming from humble beginnings, he was determined to break free from societal constraints and express his artistic genius. With limited resources, he sought opportunities to study under the tutelage of renowned masters, absorbing their techniques and craftsmanship.

One of Michelangelo's most iconic achievements was the magnificent frescoes adorning the ceiling of the Sistine Chapel at the Vatican. This ambitious project presented numerous obstacles, including the physical demands of working on a massive scale and the intricate details required to bring his vision to life.

Michelangelo encountered setbacks and frustrations along the way. The arduous process of lying on his back for extended periods, painting against gravity, and meticulously crafting each figure tested his patience and physical endurance. However, he refused to succumb to doubt or despair.

Driven by an unwavering commitment to excellence, Michelangelo embraced a growth mindset. He viewed challenges as opportunities for growth and learning. Instead of seeing setbacks as failures, he approached them with curiosity, seeking innovative solutions and refining his technique.

His relentless pursuit of perfection demanded countless hours of dedication and unwavering focus. Michelangelo's growth mindset enabled him to see each stroke of his brush as a chance to improve, each color blend as an opportunity to elevate his artistry.

Finally, after years of tireless effort, Michelangelo unveiled his masterpiece to the world. The breathtaking frescoes on the Sistine Chapel ceiling showcased the grandeur of his imagination, the precision of his craftsmanship, and the depth of his artistic vision. His work became an enduring symbol of human creativity and a testament to the power of a growth mindset.

Michelangelo's story inspires us to embrace the journey of growth and transformation. Like him, we can overcome obstacles, persist through setbacks, and continually refine our skills and abilities. Through his example, we learn the importance of nurturing a growth mindset, where challenges become stepping stones to greatness and every stroke of effort brings us closer to realizing our artistic vision.

As you navigate your own path, remember Michelangelo's unwavering commitment to growth. Embrace the challenges that come your way, view setbacks as opportunities for learning, and persistently pursue your own masterpiece. With a growth mindset, you can create timeless works of art in every aspect of your life.

Within the depths of these pages, we have explored actionable steps that empower us to embark on a personal odyssey toward abundance and success. We have delved into the realms of defining our vision, igniting our inspired action, taking consistent action, and sparking our growth potential. Along the way, we have been inspired by the stories of visionary leaders, fiery trailblazers, and artistic geniuses who have embraced these principles and transformed their lives and the world around them.

Armed with the tools and wisdom we have uncovered, you now stand on the threshold of a remarkable journey. You are called to rise above mediocrity, transcend limitations, and script a narrative that defies expectations. Through intentional and purposeful action, you breathe life into your dreams, infusing them with unwavering determination and unwavering belief.

As you embark on this journey, remember the inspiring stories of individuals who have embraced action and achieved greatness. Let their journeys inspire you to take consistent action, identifying the key steps that will propel you toward your goals. Commit to executing these actions on a regular basis, incorporating them into your daily, weekly, and monthly routines. Embrace the power of consistency, knowing that each action builds momentum and brings you closer to your desired outcomes.

Final Action

As the sun sets on this chapter, we stand at the precipice of a transformative journey, a journey that has unraveled the mysteries of action, the key that unlocks the doors to abundance and success. We have ventured into the realm of possibility, where dreams manifest into reality through deliberate and purposeful steps.

Imagine a world where each moment brims with explosive potential, where the mere whisper of an idea ignites a blaze of transformation. It is within this realm that the power of action takes hold — a force that propels us forward, urging us to leap beyond the boundaries of the ordinary and embrace the extraordinary.

Consider the tale of an ordinary individual who, with unwavering determination, unleashed the Wealth Spark within. This individual, driven by a vision of prosperity, stepped out of the shadows of doubt and into the realm of action. In ancient scriptures he embodied the essence of action and forged a path with bold strides, undeterred by challenges and fueled by an unshakable belief in his own potential.

This young man named Joseph, a dreamer with a purpose, found himself in a world plagued by envy and betrayal. His own brothers, consumed by jealousy, sold him into slavery, stripping him of his freedom and casting him into a pit of despair. Yet, even in the darkest moments of his life, Joseph refused to succumb to hopelessness. Instead, he embraced action as his guiding light — a catalyst that would transform his fate.

As a slave in a foreign land, Joseph could have easily surrendered himself to a life of complacency and resignation. But his spirit burned with a relentless determination to rise above his circumstances. With unwavering commitment, he embraced every task, no matter how menial, as an opportunity to excel and prove his worth. His actions spoke louder than words, and his dedication caught the attention of his master.

Recognizing Joseph's potential, his master entrusted him with responsibilities and elevated him to a position of authority. But Joseph's journey was far from over. Temptation and false accusations sought to derail his progress, yet his unyielding commitment to action propelled him forward. Even in the depths of a prison cell, Joseph continued to sow seeds of action, using his skills to help others while showcasing his unwavering integrity.

Through a series of remarkable events, Joseph's wisdom, foresight, and actions caught the attention of a powerful ruler who elevated him to a position of great influence, becoming a trusted adviser to the ruler himself. From the depths of slavery and imprisonment, Joseph emerged as a beacon of hope, guiding his people through a time of famine and securing their prosperity.

Joseph's story resonates deeply with us because it exemplifies the transformative power of action. Despite facing immense adversity, he never allowed himself to become a passive observer of his own life. Instead, he took decisive action, turning his setbacks into stepping stones. Through unwavering determination and an unyielding commitment to action, he transformed his circumstances.

Through Joseph's example, we learn that action is not merely a concept — it is the very essence of transformation. It is the fuel that ignites the spark of change and propels us forward, even when the odds seem insurmountable. Joseph's story reminds us that action is not limited to grand gestures or monumental leaps; it can be found in the smallest of steps and the most mundane of tasks.

In embracing action, we awaken the Wealth Spark within us — a force that propels us from where we are to the pinnacle of success. Joseph's journey teaches us that no matter the circumstances we find ourselves in, we possess the power to shape our destiny through deliberate and purposeful action. It is through action that we breathe life into our dreams, transform challenges into opportunities, and transcend the boundaries of what is possible.

As you reflect on the inspiring story of Joseph, let his unwavering commitment to action serve as a beacon of inspiration for your own transformative journey. Remember that action is the spark that ignites the power of success. Embrace action, nurture it, and let it guide you on the path to realizing your dreams.

Are you ready to follow in Joseph's footsteps and harness this transformative power of action? The choice is yours, and the potential within you is boundless. Let your actions speak volumes, and let your journey of abundance and success unfold.

The principles we explored thus far in this chapter have empowered us with the tools to navigate the winding paths of our own journey. We learned to define our vision with clarity and precision, to paint a vivid tapestry of our desires. We harnessed the transformative power of inspired action, transcended the confines of strategic planning, and allowed our inner fire to guide us. We embraced the strength of consistency, understanding that each step, no matter how small, accumulates momentum on the path to greatness. And finally, we ignited our growth potential, adopting a growth mindset and taking actionable steps that propel us toward continuous learning and expansion.

Armed with this wisdom, you now stand at the crossroads of opportunity, ready to infuse your life with these principles. Subtle shifts in your actions, fueled by the understanding that greatness lies within your grasp, will pave the way for extraordinary transformations. The power of action, unveiled within these pages, has ignited a spark that cannot be extinguished. But your journey does not end here. The story continues to unfold, and the next chapter beckons with promises of prosperity and revelation, challenging you to use this newly discovered power of action to bring an even greater unfoldment of abundance and success into your life and the lives of others.

Take a moment to reflect on these questions. Let them serve as signposts on your journey, guiding you toward a deeper exploration of the power of action. Take time to ponder them, and let your answers illuminate the path ahead. Remember, true magic lies in the implementation of what you have learned, and by embracing these questions, you take one step closer to embodying the transformative potential that action holds.

1. What specific actions can you take today to align yourself with your vision of abundance and success?

2. How can you infuse your actions with passion, creativity, and intuition to amplify their impact?

3. Are there any consistent actions or habits you need to establish or refine to ensure progress toward your goals?

4. What growth opportunities can you seek out to expand your skills, knowledge, and mindset?

5. How can you embrace challenges and setbacks as stepping stones for growth and learning?

6. Who are the individuals in your network who share your vision or possess complementary skills, and how can you collaborate with them to accelerate your progress?

7. What steps can you take to cultivate a growth mindset and reinforce positive beliefs about your abilities?

8. How can you celebrate your progress along the way and express gratitude for the support and opportunities that come your way?

CHAPTER V

LIVING A LIFE OF ABUNDANCE AND SUCCESS

This chapter covers the ingredients essential to living a life of abundance and success: mindset, gratitude, giving back, and self-care. By incorporating these components into our daily lives, we can cultivate an abundant existence across all areas.

Achieving Abundance Beyond Just Financial Wealth

Living an abundant, successful life goes far beyond financial success. It encompasses all areas of life, including health, relationships, personal growth, and spirituality. When we live a life filled with abundance and success, we experience fulfillment, prosperity, and all-around joy.

Mindset is an essential factor for a life of abundance and success. Our thoughts shape our reality, so having a negative mindset will only attract negative experiences. On the other hand, a positive mindset attracts only positive experiences. Therefore, cultivating a mindset of abundance and success requires focus on positive thoughts, affirmations, and visualization exercises.

Gratitude is another essential ingredient for a prosperous, successful life. Expressing gratitude on a daily basis helps us shift our focus from lack to abundance, thereby attracting even more blessings into our lives.

Giving back is another integral component. When we give back to others, or to groups and institutions that have supported our growth or transformation both personally and spiritually, it brings us an immense sense of fulfillment and purpose. Our giving is often returned to us in unimaginable ways. There are many ways to give back: volunteering, donating to charity, or simply helping someone in need. It is important for all of us to find ways to give back in some way.

Self-care is also a key element of abundance. By prioritizing our own health and well-being, we give ourselves more energy to pursue goals and dreams. Take care of yourself physically, mentally, and emotionally by getting enough rest, eating nutritiously, exercising regularly, and practicing self-focused activities like meditation or journaling.

In addition, living a life of abundance and success requires setting goals, developing positive relationships, and following our passions. When we have an ambitious vision for what we want to accomplish in life, taking action toward it becomes much simpler — leading us down a path that feels rewarding and meaningful.

Being true to yourself is among the most crucial steps to living a success-filled life. When our actions align with our core values and beliefs, we experience an authentic sense of fulfillment and authenticity. So it's important that you identify your core values and live your life according to them.

Achieving success requires an integrated approach that involves all areas of life. Cultivating positive attitudes, expressing gratitude, giving back, practicing self-care, setting goals that can be reached, cultivating meaningful relationships, following your passions, and being true to yourself will all help you create a life that is abundant in every aspect.

Earl Nightingale, an American radio speaker and author known for his work on self-improvement and personal development who is often referred to as the "Dean of Personal Development," once said, "We become what we think about most of the time, and that's the strangest secret." This quote emphasizes the power of our thoughts and beliefs in shaping our reality. If we focus on abundance and success, we can attract those things into our lives. However, if we constantly dwell on negativity and scarcity, we will continue to experience those things. By understanding this "strangest secret" and taking control of your thoughts, you can create a life of abundance and success beyond just financial wealth.

An abundant, successful life is not just about financial wealth. It's about having an inner sense of purpose and fulfillment in all areas of life. By taking time to reflect on your values and goals and aligning your actions with them, you can experience the joy and contentment you deserve. This could include pursuing a career aligned with passions and values, cultivating meaningful relationships with family members, engaging in hobbies or activities that bring you joy, or contributing to communities through giving, service, or volunteerism.

An abundant, successful life requires taking care of your physical and mental well-being. This includes regular exercise, healthy nutrition, self-care strategies, as well as seeking professional assistance when required. By prioritizing your health, you become better equipped to tackle challenges life throws your way and enjoy all that life has to offer — both materially and mentally!

A successful life requires cultivating an attitude of gratitude and abundance. Focusing on what you have rather than what you lack attracts more positivity and abundance into your life. Use daily gratitude, affirmations, and visualization exercises to shift your perspective profoundly toward the positive.

Living a life of abundance and success requires more than financial wealth. It requires aligning thoughts and actions with values and goals, prioritizing both physical and mental health, and cultivating an attitude of gratitude for what you have. By living this way, you can experience the joy, fulfillment, abundance, and manifested dreams that your life richly deserves.

The Importance of Gratitude, Giving, Generosity, and Serving Others

This section offers a profound exploration of success and abundance extending beyond mere financial prosperity. It uncovers the true essence of an abundant life, one that is rooted in fulfillment, purpose, and joy permeating all areas of existence. It emphasizes the role of gratitude, generosity, giving, and service to others as cardinal virtues that can enrich your life with more than material wealth.

It also provides an in-depth understanding of how cultivating a grateful heart, embracing a spirit of giving, demonstrating generosity, and serving others can become your conduits to a more meaningful, abundant life. Here is where we delve into why these elements are paramount in crafting a life teeming with success and abundance.

This illustrates that the pursuit of success is not a solitary journey. It involves uplifting others and sharing your bounty. The gratification derived from giving and serving resonates far deeper and lasts much longer than any material gain. This aspect of abundance magnifies our successes and intensifies our joy, making our lives richer in the most profound sense. Let's take a closer look.

Gratitude is an immensely powerful force that can drastically change lives. It allows us to appreciate what we have and shift our focus from lacking to appreciating what we already possess. Gratitude also helps foster a positive outlook, which attracts more abundance and success into our lives. G. K. Chesterton (1874–1936), a celebrated English writer, philosopher, and theologian, regarded as one of the most influential writers of his time, famously said, "I would maintain that thanks are the highest form of thought and that gratitude is happiness doubled by wonder."

Mindfulness is one of the best ways to cultivate gratitude. Being mindful involves being fully present in the moment and appreciating its beauty. By engaging all five senses, we can connect with this present moment and find joy in even life's simplest things. As Eckhart Tolle once said, "Realize deeply that this present moment is all you ever have; make it your primary focus throughout your life."

Another way to cultivate gratitude is keeping a gratitude journal. This helpful tool allows us to record daily the things we are thankful for, which shifts our focus away from what we lack toward what we already possess and encourages us to have an upbeat outlook on life. As American author and speaker Louise Hay once said, "Gratitude has the power to shift your energy and attract more of what you desire into your life; be grateful for what you already have, and you'll attract even more good things!"

Giving and generosity are fundamental to living an abundant life. By giving to others, we make an impact on the world around us and experience feelings of fulfillment and purpose. Giving can take many forms, whether it's volunteering your time, providing donations to charity, or offering assistance to someone in need. Giving is an inherent part of the human experience and a fundamental aspect of living a worthwhile and meaningful life. Albert Einstein beautifully said, "Only a life lived for others is a life worthwhile."

Giving and generosity can also attract more abundance, prosperity, and success. As American author and speaker Zig Ziglar famously said, "If you help enough people get what they want, you will eventually get what you desire."

There are numerous stories of individuals who have found abundance and success through giving back and serving others. Warren Buffett, one of the wealthiest individuals in the world, has earned a reputation for his philanthropic efforts and has donated billions of dollars to numerous causes and charities. Through his generosity, he has not only assisted others but also drawn more abundance and success into his own life. Buffett has pledged to donate more than 99% of his wealth to charitable causes, believing that "If you're among the fortunate 1 percent, it is your obligation to think about those less fortunate." Buffett's donations have gone toward education, health care, poverty relief, and more. He has also served as an example for others to give back, encouraging fellow billionaires to donate at least half their wealth through "The Giving Pledge." Through his generosity, Buffett not only made a lasting impact on the world but also experienced personal fulfillment and joy in return.

Giving is fundamental to a life of abundance and success, with the power to transform not only those to whom we give but also ourselves. Oprah Winfrey is an inspiring example of someone who has found abundance through giving; her generosity not only helped others but also brought greater success into her own life.

Deepak Chopra, author, public speaker, and alternative medicine advocate who is best known for his books on spirituality and mind-body medicine, such as *The Seven Spiritual Laws of Success* and *Ageless Body, Timeless Mind*, once said, "If you want joy, give joy to others; if you want love, learn to give love; if you want attention and appreciation, learn to give attention and appreciation; if you want wealth, give... help others prosper." This quote highlights the idea that giving is not only about providing material or tangible things to others but also about sharing intangible qualities such as joy, love, attention, and appreciation. By giving these qualities freely to others, we not only help them feel good, but we also invite them to reciprocate and give back to us, which ultimately brings us joy, love, and appreciation in return. It also suggests that giving to others and helping them prosper can also lead to our own prosperity, success, and abundance. When we help others achieve their goals and aspirations, we create a positive ripple effect that benefits not only them but also ourselves, as we are all interconnected. Therefore, the act of giving is not only a selfless act of kindness but also a means to bring joy, love, and prosperity into our own lives.

Numerous studies have demonstrated the beneficial effects of giving on our overall happiness. A study published in the *Journal of Social Psychology* discovered that those who spent money on others experienced greater joy than those who spent it on themselves. Another study conducted by the National Institutes of Health revealed that volunteering was linked to lower rates of depression and longer life expectancies.

American entrepreneur and philanthropist John Paul DeJoria, best known as the co-founder of the Paul Mitchell line of hair products and The Patrón Spirits Company, famously said, "Success without sharing is failure." When we have resources like time or money to give away, it is our obligation to spread them around.

In addition to giving, cultivating an attitude of gratitude and generosity is essential for living an abundant life. American author Melody Beattie noted, "Gratitude unlocks life's fullness; it turns what we have into enough, turns denial into acceptance, chaos into order, confusion into clarity — it can transform a meal into a feast, transform a house into a home — even turn strangers into friends!"

By cultivating gratitude, we cultivate a positive outlook that attracts abundance and success into our lives. We begin to view the world differently, being able to recognize and appreciate all of life's blessings that surround us.

Generosity is another cardinal virtue for living a fulfilling life. Being generous allows us to receive even more blessings in return. As Winston Churchill eloquently stated, "We make a living by what we get, but we make a life by what we give." This powerful quote underlines the reciprocal nature of generosity and the profound impact it has on our journey toward abundance and success.

Serving others is also an integral part of living a successful life. Not only does serving others benefit us personally, but it also allows us to grow as individuals by developing empathy, compassion, and an insight into the world around us. American theologian Richard J. Foster famously said, "To serve someone else is like ministering to Christ himself — taking up His yoke and learning from Him. In serving others, we become like Him."

As you can see, serving others is another catalyst to an abundant life. This is because true abundance and success can only arrive through the fulfillment of purposeful service to others. Not only do we help those around us, but doing so also allows us to grow exponentially. Through service we can foster greater empathy, compassion, and a better appreciation for all its beauty.

Oprah Winfrey, media mogul and philanthropist, famously said, "The biggest adventure you can ever take is to live the life of your dreams." When we serve others, we not only help them achieve their dreams, but we also help ourselves achieve our own. Serving others allows us to tap into our full potential and realize the power we have to make a positive impact on the world. By living a life of service, we can experience the true joy and fulfillment that comes with making a difference in the lives of others and, ultimately, achieve our own dreams and goals.

The significance of giving, gratitude, generosity, and serving others has been stressed throughout history in religious texts and inspirational books. The following quotes from *The Prosperity Bible* can be applied to modern-day prosperity and success.

"Let each man learn the law of giving and receiving, and he will prosper in everything he does." —*Wallace D. Wattles*

"If you want to receive, then you must give — this is the principle of the universe." —*John Templeton*

"The more you give, the greater reward comes back to you" —*Randy Gage*

"God is the greatest giver in the universe and He will never let you outgive Him." —*Randy Gage*

These quotes emphasize the significance of giving and serving others as a way to attract more abundance and success into our lives. When we give from a place of abundance with an authentic desire to help others, we open ourselves up to receiving even greater blessings and abundance in return.

There are countless stories of individuals who have found abundance and success through giving back and serving others. Bill Gates, for instance, has dedicated much of his wealth to charitable causes through the Bill and Melinda Gates Foundation. By their actions, not only have the Gateses improved lives around the world, but they have also inspired others to give back in similar ways.

In the quest for a life filled with abundance and success, we often overlook the powerful role of gratitude, giving, generosity, and service to others. These virtues hold the key to a life of fulfillment that extends beyond material wealth, infusing every moment with joy and a deep sense of purpose.

Countless stories echo this truth, the stories of everyday heroes whose lives are filled with richness and satisfaction, not simply from the abundance they accumulated but from the lives they touched and the difference they made. These are people who understand that true prosperity is measured not by what we get but by what we give.

As an example, consider the compelling study by professors Michael Norton and Elizabeth Dunn titled "Prosocial Spending and Happiness: Using Money to Benefit Others Pays Off." The findings of their research support the idea that spending money on others, or prosocial spending, can increase people's happiness. This suggests that the act of giving — whether in terms of time, effort, or resources — is not just beneficial for the receivers. It also brings about increased happiness and satisfaction for the giver.

Cultivating a lifestyle that centers around gratitude, giving, and serving others can significantly contribute to our overall sense of success and fulfillment. This underscores the idea that real prosperity is not just about acquiring wealth but also about enriching the lives of others. As we nurture these values in our daily routines, we pave the way for a life of true abundance and success.

A successful life is not just about what we can accumulate for ourselves; it's about what we can give to others. American writer and motivational speaker Denis Waitley famously said, "The winner's edge is not in genetics or talent — it's all in attitude!" Attitude truly is the criterion for success." By cultivating an attitude of gratitude, giving, generosity, and service toward others, we can make an impact on the world around us and experience true abundance — far beyond material possessions.

Patagonia, the popular outdoor clothing and gear company, is renowned for their high-quality products as well as their commitment to environmental conservation. They have a long history of giving back to the planet with initiatives such as donating 1 percent of sales to environmental causes and promising 100 percent of Black Friday sales to grassroots environmental organizations.

Patagonia encourages employees to give back through a program called "Earth Service Corps." This initiative offers paid time off for employees to volunteer for environmental causes, and has proven highly successful at cultivating an internal culture of giving and environmental stewardship within the company.

As Yvon Chouinard, founder of Patagonia, once said, "Philanthropy comes from the Greek *philanthropos*, meaning 'love of humanity.' That is what it means to be a philanthropist — to love humanity." Patagonia's commitment to giving back to the planet is a testament to their passion for making our world a better place.

Patagonia's example demonstrates that giving back doesn't only have to involve money; it can also involve giving time, skills, and resources to causes we care about. When we give from a place of genuine love and desire for positive impact, not only do we help those in need, but we also experience a sense of fulfillment and purpose in our own lives.

Seeking Fulfillment and Purpose in Life

The journey to personal fulfillment and purpose is as diverse as humanity itself. There is no universal map or guidebook, as our unique passions, dreams, and core values carve distinct paths for each of us. Yet, amid this splendid diversity, some universally applicable strategies can serve as guiding stars, illuminating our paths toward a life brimming with purpose and satisfaction. In this exploration, we delve into these strategies, which have the potential to catalyze our quest for a richer, more meaningful life experience. These are not rigid instructions, but flexible tools that you can adapt and mold according to your personal narrative, setting you on a course toward a life of fulfillment and purpose.

Nine Strategies for Finding Fulfillment

1. Define Your Core Values

Identifying your core values is an essential first step to a fulfilling, purposeful life. These standards or principles define who you are as an individual and serve as guidelines for decision-making and goal setting. Examples of core values include honesty, integrity, compassion, creativity, and adventure — just to name a few! Aligning your goals and actions with what matters most to you will bring greater meaning into your everyday life.

To identify your core values, begin by reflecting on what matters most to you. What principles drive you? What motivates and inspires you? Once you have a list of potential values, narrow it down to those you consider most important. Use these values as a guide when setting goals, making decisions, and living an authentic life.

2. Create Meaningful Goals

Setting meaningful goals is key to finding fulfillment and purpose. Goals that are meaningful offer direction and motivation, giving you a sense of achievement when reached. But make sure the goals are aligned with your values and interests rather than focused solely on external factors like money or status.

Goals give you something to strive toward, providing direction and a sense of purpose. When setting goals and objectives, make them specific, measurable, achievable, relevant, and time-bound (SMART). Doing so ensures you are set up for success while giving yourself a road map for reaching them.

Setting meaningful goals begins by recognizing what you truly desire in your life. What are your passions and interests? If money and time were no object, what would you do if the possibilities were endless? Make a list of potential goals and then prioritize them according to their importance for you. Afterward, create an action plan by breaking each goal down into smaller, manageable steps. By this process of setting meaningful objectives and working your action plan will bring to your life an enhanced sense of purpose and accomplishment.

3. Engage in Self-reflection

Self-reflection is an effective tool for gaining clarity and perspective on your life. Reflecting on the experiences, emotions, and beliefs you hold dear allows you to gain a more profound comprehension of who you are and what matters most to you. Moreover, self-reflection helps identify patterns of behavior or thought that could hinder you from reaching your objectives or finding fulfillment in life.

Practice self-reflection by setting aside some time daily or weekly to reflect on your experiences and emotions. You can do this through journaling, meditation, or taking a few moments of silent examination. Ask yourself questions such as "What am I grateful for?" "What did I learn today?" and "What can I do differently tomorrow?" By regularly engaging in self-reflection, you will develop greater levels of self-awareness and be able to make lasting changes in your life.

4. Foster a Positive Mindset

Cultivating a positive mindset fosters a greater sense of fulfillment and life purpose. A positive outlook helps you conquer challenges, stay motivated, and see the opportunities in any situation. On the other hand, a negative outlook may hold you back, limit your potential, and make it hard to find joy or meaning in daily activities.

Cultivate a positive mindset by practicing gratitude and optimism. Reflect on the things in your life you are thankful for, then look for opportunities and solutions instead of dwelling on the negative. Surround yourself with supportive people to reinforce these concepts while limiting exposure to negativity and toxicity.

5. Find Ways to Serve Others

Serving others can be a rewarding and purposeful way to live a life of abundance and success. There are many ways we can serve, whether it's volunteering at a local charity, helping those in need, or offering someone an encouraging word during difficult times. Serving not only has positive effects on those we serve but also has beneficial effects on ourselves. By serving others, you develop empathy and compassion toward the world around you. The act of service ultimately leads you toward discovering your purpose in life, as you find fulfillment by making a positive difference in others' lives.

6. Promote Self-Care

Self-care is paramount for living an abundant, successful life. We must prioritize our physical, emotional, and mental well-being in order to live our best lives; this includes getting enough sleep, eating nutritiously, and exercising regularly. In addition, taking time for self-reflection and personal growth through reading books, attending personal development seminars, or seeking the guidance of an experienced mentor or coach are all important aspects of self-care.

7. Acknowledge and Embrace Challenges and Failures

Challenges and setbacks are inevitable parts of life, yet they can also serve as powerful opportunities for growth and development. When we embrace them, we learn valuable lessons that make us stronger and more resilient. In addition, adopting a growth mindset fosters the viewing of difficulties as chances for improvement rather than setbacks.

8. Cultivate Positive and Supportive Environments

Our environment has a profound effect on how we feel, from uplift to inspiration. Surrounding ourselves with like-minded individuals will help shape who we become at our best. Always seek out relationships with those who share your values and encourage you to reach greater heights.

9. Find Joy in the Present Moment

Finally, finding joy in the present moment is essential for a fulfilling life. While setting goals and working toward the future are necessary, taking time out of your busy life to appreciate and enjoy what you have is equally important. This could include spending quality time with loved ones, taking a walk in nature, or practicing mindfulness or meditation. These special moments will bring you joy!

Finding fulfillment and purpose is a key component of an abundant, successful life. Doing so involves finding ways to serve others, practicing self-care, setting goals and working toward them, accepting challenges and failures, surrounding ourselves with positive people who support us, and finding joy in the present moment. By implementing these strategies, you can discover your true calling and achieve lasting success and abundance in all areas of your life.

Practical Strategies for a Success Journey

Basking in the warm sun of abundance and success isn't a matter of chance or luck — it's a deliberate, vibrant dance between a mindset shift and consistent, strategic actions. This dance begins with an attitude makeover, from scarcity to abundance, from fear to courage, from self-doubt to self-belief. It's about adopting a mindset that not only dreams of success but also breathes, eats, and lives it.

However, this attitudinal transformation is only half of the journey. The other half is the physical stride, the steps we take, the actions we execute to make our goals come alive. This is not a sprint but a marathon. It's a dedication to constant progression, no matter how small each step might be.

This section delves into practical strategies and exercises you can incorporate into your life to cultivate this mindset and foster the habits that fuel consistent action. These actionable insights will serve as your compass, guiding you on your journey to an abundant and successful life.

1. Gratitude Journaling: A most powerful way to cultivate an attitude of abundance and success attraction is gratitude journaling. Every day, take a few moments to write down three to five things you are thankful for. This exercise helps you to focus on the positive elements in your life right now, which in turn attracts even more positivity and abundance into your life.

2. Visualization: Another powerful tool for goal clarity and achievement is visualization. Spend some time every day visualizing yourself having already achieved your objectives, surrounded by joy and success. This exercise will help create an inner image of the dreams you desire and motivate you to take action toward realizing them.

3. Positive Affirmations: Affirmations are key to cultivating a success mindset. Write a short list of positive affirmations that resonate with you, such as "I am worthy of success," "I attract abundance into my life," or "I am capable of achieving my goals." Repeat these affirmations daily, believing they are true.

This exercise will help shape your self-image and attract more positivity and abundance into your life.

4. **Setting Goals:** Goal setting is essential for your success journey. Define both long-term and short-term objectives, then break them into achievable steps. Write them down and review them regularly to monitor progress. This exercise will keep you focused and motivated toward reaching those milestones.

5. **Implementing Action:** Despite all the planning and preparation, action is where the proverbial rubber meets the road. Identify the action steps necessary for reaching your goals, and then take action every day until you achieve them. The daily practice will build momentum toward success, attracting even more opportunities for prosperity and abundance along the way.

6. **Self-Care:** Self-care is a necessary component of a joyful and abundant life. Make time for activities that bring you joy and relaxation, such as exercise, meditation, or spending time with loved ones. Doing so will keep you energized and focused on reaching your objectives.

7. **Giving Back:** Giving back to others not only serves your community, but it is a foolproof way to attract more abundance into your life. Find ways to give back, whether that means donating money to a charity, volunteering your time, or offering someone in need a kind word or gesture. This exercise will help create a positive impact on the world around you while drawing in greater positivity and abundance to your own life.

Jim Rohn, an American entrepreneur and motivational speaker, once said, "Success is not something you chase; it is attracted by who you become." By becoming the best version of yourself and dedicating yourself to a life of growth and contribution, you will attract all the abundance and success you desire.

Living a life of abundance and success necessitates an internal shift and commitment to taking action toward reaching your goals. By practicing gratitude journaling, visualization, positive affirmations, setting objectives, taking action, self-care, and giving back to others, you cannot help but cultivate an attitude of abundance — which in turn attracts more success and fulfillment into your life.

Making the Dream Real

How can you live an abundant, successful life?

Imagine a life teeming with abundance, a life where success is not just a distant dream but your everyday reality. Sounds incredible, doesn't it? This chapter is your compass to that dream destination. It's a gold mine for anyone who dares to aspire to such a life, illuminating the principles and techniques that underpin abundance and success.

One of the golden threads woven through this chapter has been the essence of gratitude, giving, generosity, and service to others. These are not mere words but the heartbeat of an authentically successful and abundant life. You will uncover the powerful impact of these qualities, revealing a different perspective of success — one that transcends financial wealth, touching the richness of relationships, health, and personal growth.

Use the strategies, practical exercises, and tips given here as your road map. They are actionable steps guiding you to infuse abundance and success into every facet of your life. Not simply theoretical concepts, they are practical applications you can implement starting today.

Finally, this journey is also about self-discovery. The reflection questions presented here are not just questions — they are mirrors offering you a deeper look into your life and aspirations. They urge you to ponder, to evaluate, and to act. Through these mirrors, you'll discover more about yourself and your pathway to a life draped in abundance and success. So, let's dive in and turn that vision of an abundant and successful life into your everyday reality.

1. How can practicing gratitude help you shift your focus from what you lack to what you possess?

2. How do giving and generosity shape your own sense of abundance and success?

3. How can serving others help you grow and develop as an individual?

4. How can you incorporate gratitude into your everyday life?

5. How can you make giving and generosity an integral part of your life, regardless of your current financial situation?

6. What steps can you take to uncover your own sense of purpose and fulfillment?

7. How can you utilize your skills and talents to serve others and make a positive difference in the world?

8. What practical exercises and habits can you create to live a life of abundance and success beyond financial wealth?

CHAPTER VI

BRINGING IT ALL TOGETHER

As you near the end of this transformative book, let's review the journey we embarked on together to Ignite Your Path to Abundance and Success. This journey, filled with insights and practical steps, has been like a treasure map, unveiling the secrets to creating the life you've always dreamt of.

Each chapter held its own magic. We started with the foundations, exploring the power of mindset and the critical role it plays in setting the stage for success. We then dove into the art of goal setting, revealing how a well-aimed arrow can help us hit our target of prosperity.

Healthy habits, communication, leadership, and action were our next stops. These are invaluable skills in your tool kit, enabling you not only to dream but also to lead and inspire others in this shared quest for abundance. These topics stretch across the wide spectrum of wealth creation, unearthing knowledge to help catapult you toward your desired level of wealth and prosperity.

Recap: Keys to the Journey

It's now time to assemble these puzzle pieces into a comprehensive picture. Here we encapsulate key takeaways from each chapter, distilling the essence of this knowledge journey. This is your chance to reflect, consolidate, and prepare for the path ahead.

Keep in mind that the end of this book does not mark the end of your journey. It's merely a stepping stone. Know that this is your springboard into a future brimming with abundance and success. Continue to learn, grow, and apply these lessons, transforming this knowledge into a way of life. Your path to abundance and success lies before you.

1. Foster a Growth Mindset

Embracing a growth mindset is a critical catalyst for achieving abundance and success. This involves welcoming learning, growth, and change and reframing setbacks as platforms for development instead of instances of failure. Adopting this positive perspective toward challenges allows you to face them with an optimistic mindset and a readiness to learn and adapt.

2. Establish Clear and Specific Goals

Setting clear and specific goals is a pivotal component in achieving abundance and success. This involves identifying your big-picture aspirations, breaking those goals down into measurable objectives, and devising strategies to reach them. Setting goals and objectives helps you stay focused and motivated while tracking your progress as you strive toward realizing them.

3. Foster Positive Habits

Successful individuals have often cultivated a set of beneficial routines they follow regularly, such as exercising, healthy eating, meditation, and reading. By developing positive habits like these, you can improve your overall well-being and create foundational elements for abundance and success on your journey.

4. Foster Effective Communication Skills

Effective communication is a necessary trait for success in any area of life, be it business, relationships, or personal growth. By developing strong communication abilities, you will improve your capacity to connect with others, express your ideas and opinions clearly, and navigate challenging conversations or situations more effectively.

5. Foster Successful Relationships

Success often rests upon the foundation of strong connections. Whether with business partners, colleagues, friends, or family, nurturing these connections helps people reach their objectives and find greater fulfillment and satisfaction in life. By dedicating time and energy to cultivating and maintaining these bonds and fostering like-minded relationships, you can create a support system that can help you reach the success you desire.

6. Develop Resilience and Perseverance

Achieving abundance and success is not always smooth sailing, and setbacks and difficulties will inevitably occur along the way. But by cultivating resilience and perseverance, you can more easily navigate these difficulties while continuing your forward progress. This means being able to bounce back from setbacks, stay focused on what matters most, and never give up on your dreams or aspirations.

7. Continue to Learn and Grow

The journey to abundance and success is a lifelong quest. By constantly learning, you can stay abreast of your industry and interest, adjust according to changing circumstances, and discover new opportunities for development. This involves seeking out knowledge, attending conferences and events, as well as continuing personal and professional growth activities.

8. Take Bold and Consistent Action

One crucial element that must not be overlooked on the journey to abundance and success is the power of taking bold and consistent action. All the mindset shifts, goal setting, habits, communication skills, relationships, resilience, and learning mean little if they are not accompanied by action. Action is the catalyst that brings ideas to life, propels you forward, and transforms dreams into reality.

To truly manifest abundance and success, you must be willing to step outside your comfort zone and take calculated risks. Embrace the power of inspired action, fueling it with passion, creativity, and intuition. Let each step you take be purposeful, aligned with your goals, and driven by unwavering determination.

The key to achieving abundance and success is a combination of mindset, habits, skills, relationships, and actions. By adopting a growth mindset, setting clear and specific goals, cultivating positive habits, mastering effective communication techniques, building strong connections, practicing resilience and perseverance, continuously learning and growing, and taking bold and consistent action, you can ignite your path to abundance and success.

In the pages of this book, you now have a comprehensive framework for creating a life of abundance, success, meaning, purpose, and fulfillment. Included is a full array of actionable strategies and techniques — from setting clear intentions and cultivating a growth mindset to taking consistent action — each designed to ignite your potential.

Keep in mind that the key to abundance and success lies within each individual. By acknowledging and releasing limiting beliefs while simultaneously fostering a growth mindset, you can unlock your infinite potential. This transformation, coupled with the application of the principles and tactics outlined in this book, is the first step on your path to the life you truly desire.

Nelson Mandela, the renowned South African anti-apartheid revolutionary, political leader, and philanthropist, once said, "There is no passion to be found playing small — in settling for a life that is less than the one you are capable of living."

This Mandela quote emphasizes the power within each person to live a full and meaningful life. It encourages individuals to reject mediocrity, to embrace their potential, and to aspire to the greatness that lies within them. Just as the passage indicates, by acknowledging and overcoming limiting beliefs, and by fostering a growth mindset, individuals can unlock their immense potential, enabling them to lead lives filled with abundance and success. By continuously seeking to grow and improve, we make ourselves magnets for success and prosperity.

The Wealth Spark: Igniting Your Path to Abundance and Success has been your guide to the successful pursuit of abundance in all areas of life. Through mindset shifts, practical strategies, and actionable tips, it has invited you to embark on a journey toward a life filled with purpose, fulfillment, and abundance. You have been encouraged to adopt a growth mindset, create a clear vision, and take consistent action steps to unlock and ignite your full potential, setting you on the path to create the life you truly desire.

Keep in mind, however, that true abundance and success do not come simply from financial wealth or material possessions. They derive instead from living a life with purpose, meaning, and fulfillment while making an impact on those around us.

As Steve Jobs once said, "Your work will take up a significant part of your life — the only way to truly be fulfilled is to do what you believe to be excellent work. And the only way to love what you do is by finding fulfillment within yourself." If you haven't found it yet, keep searching — don't settle. As with all matters of the heart, you'll know when you find it."

AFTERWORD

In the pages of *The Wealth Spark: Igniting Your Path to Abundance and Success* are woven together a multitude of ideas, strategies, and insights to guide you on your journey to a life of profound abundance. Not just a compilation of random thoughts, the book has given you a comprehensive framework that draws from the wellsprings of diverse disciplines, bridging the gap between ambition and achievement, dreams and reality.

The ideas presented are not conjured out of thin air. They are grounded in credible research, studies, and the wisdom of accomplished thought leaders from various fields. To ensure the richness of the content and solidify your trust, dear reader, we have made it a priority to back up our assertions with credible, scholarly references.

The reference list below presents a treasure trove of additional resources, providing a wide-ranging buffet of thought and research. They are like a road map into the minds of the greatest thinkers and achievers in the realms of personal development, wealth creation, and success. Included are insightful books, engaging articles, thought-provoking statements made during interviews, and groundbreaking research studies.

These references stand as a testament to the diligence we put into the crafting of this guidebook. It underscores our commitment to offer you a body of work that is not only engaging and practical but also meticulously researched and factually sound. We hope it will not only enrich your reading experience but also inspire you to delve deeper into the fascinating, ever-evolving world of abundance and success dynamics.

References

7 Habits of Highly Effective People: Powerful Lessons in Personal Change, Stephen Covey

A Return to Love: Reflections on the Principles of A Course in Miracles, Marianne Williamson

Atomic Habits: An Easy & Proven Way to Build Good Habits & Break Bad Ones, J. Clear

Deep Work: Rules for Focused Success in a Distracted World, C. Newport

Drive: The Surprising Truth About What Motivates Us, D. H. Pink

Flow: The Psychology of Optimal Experience, M. Csikszentmihalyi

Give and Take: A Revolutionary Approach to Success, A. Grant

Grit: The Power of Passion and Perseverance, A. Duckworth

Man's Search for Meaning, Viktor E. Frankl

Maximum Achievement: Strategies and Skills That Will Unlock Your Hidden Powers to Succeed, B. Tracy

Mindset: The New Psychology of Success, C. S. Dweck

Outliers: The Story of Success, Malcolm Gladwell

Prosocial Spending and Happiness: Using Money to Benefit Others Pays Off, Michael Norton and Elizabeth Dunn

The 21 Irrefutable Laws of Leadership: Follow Them and People Will Follow You, J. C. Maxwell

The Millionaire Next Door, Thomas J. Stanley and William Danko

The Power of Positive Thinking, Norman Vincent Peale

The Psychology of Money, Morgan Housel

The Richest Man in Babylon, George S. Clason

The Science of Getting Rich, Wallace D. Wattles

The Seven Spiritual Laws of Success, Deepak Chopra

Think and Grow Rich, Napoleon Hill

Time magazine, September 12–19, 2022, Serena Williams (Cover)

Tools of Titans: The Tactics, Routines, and Habits of Billionaires, Icons, and World-Class Performers, T. Ferriss

Unshakeable: Your Financial Freedom Playbook, T. Robbins

You Are a Badass: How to Stop Doubting Your Greatness and Start Living an Awesome Life, J. Sincero

In addition to these sources, many other books, articles, and research studies are cited throughout to further elaborate upon the ideas presented. Consult these references to gain a better understanding of the topics addressed in this book and discover additional resources to continue your personal development journey.

ABOUT THE AUTHOR

Reverend James C. Parker, an ordained Unity minister and the senior minister of Unity Chicago, has been at the helm of executive church management for over twenty years. As a renowned agent of transformation, his inspirational leadership and dynamic public speaking skills have fostered a culture of shared values, ethics, and diversity, advancing organizational objectives.

Rev. Parker's expertise spans a wide range of areas, from strategic planning and staff management to communications and special projects. A visionary, he is adept at charting comprehensive strategic plans, fostering key partnerships, and coordinating initiatives that lead to the operational growth and well-being of the church. As an administrative leader, he excels in building relationships and implementing church policy, ensuring a seamless operational flow.

An accomplished business professional, Rev. Parker has extended his influence beyond the pulpit to the realms of retail, hospitality, and government contracting. He has also held the role of president and CEO of a business consulting firm, where he honed his skills in strategic planning, business development, staff training, and financial management.

A lifelong learner and teacher, Rev. Parker holds a bachelor of arts degree in liberal arts with minors in communications and marketing. He completed his theological training at Unity Institute and Seminary, Unity Urban Ministerial School, and Unity School of Christianity. His educational background has given him a solid foundation for teaching various subjects, including spiritual enrichment, metaphysics, Bible interpretation, prosperity principles, prayer, and Christian healing.

Aside from his official duties, Rev. Parker's dedication extends to volunteer activities like serving on the Board of Trustees at Unity World Headquarters, contributing to local hospitals and libraries, and fundraising for The United Way.

Because Parker was endowed with a profound spiritual intellect, his literary interests include writing and reading across genres, with a special focus on self-help, spiritual development, nonfiction, and poetry. An ardent devotee of lifelong learning, his other passions include golf, swimming, running, ministering, chaplaincy, pastoral counseling, life coaching, and music.

Reverend James C. Parker brings all this rich experience and wisdom to the pages of *The Wealth Spark*, aiming to empower readers to unlock their potential and create abundant, fulfilling lives.

Printed in the USA
CPSIA information can be obtained
at www.ICGtesting.com
LVHW022047250124
769470LV00073B/1847